Britain at War 1939 to 1945

What was life like during the war?

by

James Lingard

authorHOUSE®

AuthorHouse™ UK Ltd.
500 Avebury Boulevard
Central Milton Keynes, MK9 2BE
www.authorhouse.co.uk
Phone: 08001974150

© 2008 James Lingard. All rights reserved.

No part of this book may be reproduced, stored in a retrieval system, or transmitted by any means without the written permission of the author.

First published by AuthorHouse 4/11/2008

ISBN: 978-1-4343-5934-6 (e)
ISBN: 978-1-4343-5933-9 (sc)

Printed in the United States of America
Bloomington, Indiana

This book is printed on acid-free paper.

Contents

Introduction		*vii*
Chapter 1	*Life Pre-war*	*1*
Chapter 2	*War Is Declared*	*10*
Chapter 3	*My First Bomb*	*20*
Chapter 4	*Battle Of Britain*	*25*
Chapter 5	*On The Move*	*35*
Chapter 6	*Village Life*	*42*
Chapter 7	*Isle Of Man*	*49*
Chapter 8	*Barbarossa*	*57*
Chapter 9	*The Americans Declare War*	*65*
Chapter 10	*1942*	*70*
Chapter 11	*The Desert*	*76*
Chapter 12	*Russia*	*84*
Chapter 13	*Italy*	*88*
Chapter 14	*Far East*	*96*
Chapter 15	*D-day*	*102*
Chapter 16	*The Battle For Europe*	*111*
Chapter 17	*The Home Front*	*115*
Chapter 18	*Victory*	*120*
Epilogue		*128*

This book is dedicated to all those who suffered on the road to victory and in particular to my parents.

Introduction

This history of the Second World War is written as far as possible from the standpoint of people actually involved so that the reader can obtain an insight into their hopes and fears and an idea of what it was like to live in Britain during the war. History is more interesting if brought to life, and the Second World War had countless dramas and moments of real fear for those who lived at that time.

Imagine strolling along the Brighton promenade in the sunshine when, without warning, a German fighter returning to France dives out of the blue and empties its machine guns at the passers-by. My brother-in-law will never forget. Death could come out of nowhere at any time.

However, facts and figures given are historically accurate rather than the propaganda fed to a public desperately in need of reassurance. This is not to deny the value of being selective with the truth at the time of such crises as the aftermath of Dunkirk, or the need to conceal military information from the enemy.

Britain had been gravely damaged by the First World War and people were strongly opposed to reliving the suffering yet again - a horror still fresh in their memory after a mere twenty years. That War had cost around ten million lives - 800,000 of them British - and many more crippled, but victory had not brought happiness. Britain remained far from a land fit for heroes which the soldiers had been promised. People questioned whether all this had been worthwhile.

There was a real danger for a time that the Russian revolution might spread here. Troops became restive at the delay in demobilising them - fearing that the Government might send them to fight the Bolsheviks. Then again there was no work for them, and in many cases not even homes.

The war had cost an estimated forty thousand million pounds in sterling worth far more than the pound today; a national debt which the Government was reluctant to increase by launching much needed housing and other projects at the taxpayers' expense. In the end, the unemployment and poverty led to riots and a series of major damaging strikes - the railways, the miners, the shipyards and many other industries - culminating in the General strike of 1926; but no revolution.

The adversity caused by the General strike resulted in a great patriotic response which weakened the unions and the outlook briefly improved, until any hope of prosperity was dashed by the Stock Market crash in the United States which rumbled round the world. This caused unemployment and poverty to continue in Britain through the 1930s, until the country began belatedly to rearm. Unemployment had fallen to 1.7 million in 1938 and all but disappeared by the end of the war.

The economic problems of the 1920s, culminating in the Great Crash on 21st October 1929, stemmed from the massive war debts, which had imposed an intolerable strain on the world's economies. The crippling repayments to the United States gave the appearance of increasing prosperity in that country, leading to an orgy of optimism and speculation based on cheap credit. Economists, bankers and the stock market persuaded themselves that economic cycles were a thing of the past - rather as they have done recently.

In 2007, Britain finally repaid to the United States the war debts arising from the Second World War. Again, we have seen optimism and speculation based on cheap credit. Will the Authorities be more successful in managing today's markets? This time, they seem inclined to reduce interest rates to stave off a crisis; rather than increase them to protect the value of the currency.

And why did the optimism and speculation suddenly end in 1929? In 1925, Britain had restored its currency to the gold standard at the pre-war rate - a rate which at that time seriously overvalued the pound, thereby damaging exporters and increasing already high unemployment and industrial unrest. Imperial pride refused to accept that its economy had been weakened by the war.

Gold began to flow in a steady and increasing stream to New York which was also on the gold standard. This had to be reversed, and it was on 26th September 1929 when the Bank of England dramatically raised its Base Rate by one per cent to 6.5% - a move followed by a number of other countries. This forced the United States to increase its own interest rates with devastating consequences for speculators and members of the public who had overextended themselves relying on cheap loans.

One other factor of general significance was the improvement in the position of women. So many men had perished in the war that women had and took their chance to show what they could do. The suffragettes won them the vote, but war work had demonstrated that women were at least as capable as men in less physical jobs and they saw no reason not to continue in those jobs when the war ended. This, of course, was one of the factors which exacerbated unemployment.

Britain's rigid class structure somehow survived the First World War. This and corrupting nepotism held her back. The public schools continued to produce the leaders of the nation. The wealthy and the aristocracy lived in luxury, though not to the same extent as before the war. They - like everyone else - had relatives and friends killed and wounded. They too suffered from a paucity of eligible bachelors. Then again, servants were harder to come-by and more expensive. The returning heroes had seen something of the world and were no longer prepared to spend their lives as servants. And then came the crash, which ruined many, though not the landed gentry.

The three million unemployed and their families were at the opposite end of the scale. Unemployment benefit was but a dream for the future; starvation a real threat. There were hunger marches to draw their plight to the attention of the nation. The incompetent generals of the so called Great War were never brought to account; while shell shocked troops had been shot as cowards. A sense of injustice - of inability to achieve one's full potential - produced not merely socialists, but communists and fascists in our midst.

Even so, in 1939 the country rose up and once again fought for freedom with a steadfastness and courage which future generations can only applaud. Moreover, Britain still had the unswerving support of a powerful Empire.

Did we really declare war for Poland? If so, we failed for Stalin's oppression of that people was little better than Hitler's. On the other hand, with hindsight, the timing of the war proved to be near perfect for Britain. Any earlier and we would not have had enough Spitfires to beat off the German air offensive against us. Any later and Hitler would have been able to bring into mass production the secret weapons his scientists did develop.

One thing which will strike the reader is how close the Allies came to disaster on a number of occasions. Fortunately, Hitler insisted on imposing strategy on his Generals and he made serious errors of judgment against their advice. Churchill also would have made some errors, but each time he was overruled either by the War Cabinet or by his Allies. His true greatness was not as a strategist, but as a leader who held together a defeated army after Dunkirk, inspired his people, and led them to victory. He also held the Allies together during times of crisis - no easy task given that America, Russia and Britain had very different objectives once Hitler was defeated.

* * *

CHAPTER 1

Life Pre-war

'I hold in my hand a piece of paper which bears Herr Hitler's signature as well as mine.' *(Chamberlain 30th September 1938).* **And what did this piece of paper say?**

'We, the German Fuehrer and Chancellor and the British Prime Minister, have had a further meeting today, and are agreed in recognising that the question of Anglo-German relations is of the first importance for the two countries and for Europe. We regard the agreement signed last night and the Anglo-German Naval Agreement as symbolic as the desire of our two peoples never to go to war with one another again. We are resolved that the method of consultation shall be the method adopted to deal with any other question that may concern our two countries, and we are determined to continue our efforts to remove possible sources of difference and thus to contribute to the assurance of peace in Europe.'

Chamberlain interpreted this as 'peace for our time' - something overwhelmingly desired by a war weary nation still struggling to come to terms with the death and destruction of the First World War, 'the war to end all wars'.

Why did Hitler agree? Von Ribbentrop, then German Ambassador to Britain, had sought an Anglo-

German alliance the year before. After all the Angles and the Saxons were both Germanic tribes and the British Royal family had Hanoverian ancestry. He proposed that Britain should give Germany a free hand in Eastern Europe - nothing more was asked of her, except perhaps the return of German colonies taken from her by the armistice.

If Britain had allowed herself to be seduced by this easy option, Hitler would probably have marched into Russia - as he did in June 1941 - instead of France. Would he have won? Be that as it may, Britain would have been sucked into war when Germany/Italy closed in on Egypt and the Suez Canal or failing that when Japan attacked Singapore/Pearl Harbour. If Russia had succumbed, no one trusted the Nazis not to renege on their promises and attack us anyhow. She had already on more than one occasion breached the arms and territorial limitations imposed on her by the treaty of Versailles.

From a British standpoint, the annexation of further territories by Hitler was utterly unacceptable. Austria, the Sudeten land and Czechoslovakia were taken over in rapid succession. Germany was growing stronger by the day and in danger of becoming unstoppable.

But in 1938, Britain was in no shape to take on Germany. We had a strong navy to defend our island from invasion, but even this was woefully exposed to torpedo bombers as the attack by Stuka dive bombers on Scapa Flow early in the war was soon to demonstrate. The fleet air arm had no modern planes capable of evading the fighters of the Luftwaffe. The RAF had five squadrons of Hurricanes and no Spitfires in service. In contrast, the Germans had over 900 fighters (including Messerschmitt 109s) and approximately 1,500 bombers, whose effectiveness had been amply demonstrated in the Spanish civil war. We comforted ourselves that these planes were all short range and little danger to us as long as France stood. If war came, we would reinforce France, though the French army by itself was believed strong enough to hold the Germans in check.

Then again our army was a fraction of the size needed to make an impact in Europe and woefully short of equipment, particularly machine guns and effective anti- aircraft guns. Our tanks - an invention of the British - might be a match for the Italians, but did not compare with the heavy tanks for the Panzer Divisions being produced in Germany. Even at the outbreak of war, the British army of 897,000 men was less than a fifth the size of the French. By 1945, it had gradually been built up to nearly three million. However, only roughly two thirds of these saw service on the battle fronts overseas.

People were divided about what to do. A minority saw war as inevitable and was impatient for the country to rearm. Most were pacifist and considered rearmament would only provoke an arms race. In any event, Germany would have to overwhelm France before she could attack Britain and that she had failed to do in World War 1. They encouraged the Government to follow a policy of appeasement. This thinking is the reason why our armed forces were in such poor shape in 1938.

James Lingard

Chamberlain himself may have believed 'peace in our time', but it did not deter him from rearming using every resource available. As an illustration, by the outbreak of war Britain had 300 Spitfires in service - a number which had grown to 1,000 by the start of the Battle of Britain. Even more Hurricanes were produced, not to mention air raid shelters for civilians, the radar screen and the start of conscription in April 1939. Conscription had to build up gradually over a two year period because there were insufficient weapons available for more troops. Only in 1938 did industry begin to be put on a war footing.

* * *

So much for the big picture, but what was life really like for the general population? Very different from life today. I can best illustrate this from the life style of my own family - not that they were typical of the whole country, but they speak for the areas where they lived.

My grandfather on my father's side - like many others of his generation - had left school at the age of ten, able to read and write and do simple arithmetic, but with little knowledge of history or the world outside the mill town of Hebden Bridge in the West Riding of Yorkshire where he had been born. Now, something of a beauty spot; then thriving with clothing factories, a dye works which turned the river red, and an asbestos factory which silently poisoned the almost exclusively white population.

Grandfather saw around him exploitation and poverty. He refused to submit and became one of the early members of the trade union for the clothing industry, quickly becoming a shop steward and rising to district convener responsible for the whole of Hebden Bridge. In that capacity, he led the first strike the town had ever seen - achieving a small rise in the hourly rate which the mill girls received.

There was another side to him. He was no mean tenor soloist and won many competitions as such - even being accorded the honour of singing solo before the King at the Albert Hall. At Christmas, he would tour the local chapels singing solos from Handel's Messiah. This gift broadened his horizons. He came to know a little of London, which amazed him. How could such a city survive with so few mills, so little industry?

By 1930, he had become a local celebrity. But Hebden Bridge was not immune to the catastrophic slump and unemployment which hit the nation. Things became so bad that the clothing factories only had work for one day a week, not enough hours work to feed a family. Starvation threatened. The workforce looked to him.

Grandfather notified the media that if they attended the men's clothing department at a certain store in Leeds at 11am the following Saturday, he would ensure they had a story which needed to be told. True to his word, at the appointed time with the support of some shop stewards from his Union, he sprang on to a counter at the store and addressed the astonished customers to the effect: People of Leeds, this store is selling foreign goods, depriving your fellow countrymen of work. Buy British.

James Lingard

The store manager appeared and assured everyone that they would love to buy British, but the goods were too expensive. People could not afford to pay more than absolutely necessary.

The press was interested. The union men pledged to match the foreign prices if they knew how much. Grandfather insisted on being given the key figures in writing and egged on by the reporters refused to leave until he had them.

Life is not so easy. Management in Hebden Bridge said there was no way they could match the prices. 'How much would we have to cut our wages?' grandfather demanded. Cut wages! Such a thing was unheard of then as now.

Grandfather called a mass meeting. 'If you work one day a week at today's wages, you starve and your families starve. It's as simple as that. If you work four days a week at the reduced wages, you eat, with enough over for a pint or two. Which is it to be?' He won the vote by a big margin. The contract was signed and carried on right through the depression up to the outbreak of war.

What was grandfather's lifestyle? All his married life until his death at the age of 82, he lived in the same terrace house, half way up a steep hill overlooking the river and the dye works. It boasted a sizeable kitchen dominated by a large washing machine, topped by a pair of rollers for squeezing water out of the clean clothes. Grandmother spent every Monday washing and ironing at that machine for the entire family.

She also supervised the shopping - which true to socialist traditions had to be from the local co-operative society - and general household expenditure. Not that she ever really knew how much grandfather earned, or what he did with his money. He was the master of his household to a far greater extent than would have been tolerated a generation later.

The kitchen opened on to the compact living room with a coal fire and an Aga stove for cooking. No central heating, but the fire was kept hot enough with logs or coal to heat the room. All meals were eaten at the table in this room, starting with breakfast which in grandfather's case consisted of a pint mug of strong coffee, taken early enough for him to be at work no later than 8am.

On Sundays, the whole family would attend one of the local Methodist chapels. There were several of these thanks to the efforts of John Wesley who had preached in what had been a godless area a century before. Then roast beef and roast potatoes for lunch. The family ate well, but simple locally produced food.

The house also had a front room (lounge) which was normally left unheated and only used to entertain strangers or for singing practice or on rare occasions to listen to the powerful radio -wireless set as it used to be called - which it contained. TV had not been invented. Most people went to the Cinema at least once a week. The house always had electricity and main drainage, unlike some in the vicinity which had to use an outside toilet.

All friends or relatives entered the house through the kitchen, the door of which was always open except at night, and penetrated no further than the living room. A constant flow of neighbours called unannounced for a cup of tea and a chat. This was a friendly neighbourhood where few strangers ventured.

Apart from grandmother who suffered from a bad leg, the family spent little time at home. Up early, working late, music practice and social engagements filled the time. Social engagements included the pub in the early years, until grandfather was prevailed upon - like many others - to sign the pledge. This did not prevent him keeping a bottle or two of port in the cellar, which assisted in motivating him to fill the coal scuttle.

All the mill towns had a wakes (holiday) week - always the same week but different weeks for different towns so that resorts like Blackpool could cope with the influx. Grandfather took us all to St Annes-on-sea year after year, except for his daughter Annie who regularly went with a party of friends to Switzerland.

Annie was perhaps more typical of her generation than the rest of the family. A teenager when the First World War broke out, she never married - Hebden Bridge lost heroes like the rest of the country. As a hobby, she joined the light opera society and regularly performed Gilbert and Sullivan.

My father, in his early days, became a crack shot with a pea shooter, and had the misfortune to score a number of direct hits on a worthy gentleman who years later turned out to be my mother's father. No wonder her family regarded him as a street urchin!

Father, however, inherited the work ethic and won a scholarship to the local grammar school in Halifax, passed his Matriculation and became a junior in the local branch of Lloyds Bank. This undemanding position gave him time to take a correspondence course which led to a Batchelor of Commerce degree at London University, passed with such distinction that he was awarded a Fulbright scholarship to Harvard University.

The promise of a year in the United States and a permanent escape from Halifax was enough to persuade my mother to marry him, despite the disapproval of her middle class parents. Class mattered in those days. Father learned the basics of American banking practice and had articles published in the Institute of Bankers magazine. This brought him to the attention of Lloyds Bank's senior management and led to promotion and Head Office in London.

The outbreak of war found mother, father and me living in a rented semi-detached house in Petts Wood, South London - a dormitory town very different from Hebden Bridge and not the safest of venues in the coming holocaust!

* * *

CHAPTER 2

War Is Declared

Britain and France had guaranteed the integrity of Poland in an effort to deter Hitler from invading that country, a nation which had substantial industrial and military strength - sufficient to tilt the balance of power against them. The ruse failed. On the 1st September 1939, German troops invaded Poland.

Britain served an ultimatum on Germany in the following terms:-

> **Sir:- In the communication which I had the honour to make to you on September 1, I informed you on the instructions of His Majesty's Principal Secretary of State for Foreign Affaires that unless the German Government were prepared to give his Majesty's Government in the United Kingdom satisfactory assurances that the German Government had suspended all aggressive action against Poland and were prepared promptly to withdraw their forces from Polish territory, his Majesty's Government in the United Kingdom would without hesitation fulfil their obligations to Poland.**
>
> **Although it is now more than twenty-four hours ago no reply has been received, and German attacks on Poland have continued and intensified.**
>
> **I have therefore to inform you that unless not later that 11a.m. British Summer Time to-day, September 3, satisfactory assurances to the above effect have been given by the German Government and have reached his Majesty's Government in London: a state of war would exist between the two countries as from that hour.**

Chamberlain broadcast to the Nation at 11.15am, explaining the situation in a flat monotone, strikingly devoid of any emotion. He ended: 'No such undertaking has been received by the time stipulated and consequently this country is now at war with Germany.' 'God Save the King' - which followed those fateful words - evoked deep emotion, seeming to be a chilling appeal to the Almighty for help, help the Nation sorely needed.

In my family, the broadcast was listened to in total silence. Father had expected war and looked grave, but said nothing as he switched off the radio. Mother, a pacifist, exploded in righteous indignation, as she held back her tears, to the effect: 'One minute it's peace in our time and now he declares war over Poland. How dare he? He's ruined the whole country - condemned us all to live in hell and pay the price. Who cares about Poland? Where is it anyway? What is to become of us?'

That of course was the question. What indeed. They resolved to carry on as normal until events forced them to do otherwise. What else could they do? Stock up with tinned food - there were no such things as household refrigerators or deep freezers. Fresh food had to be kept in a well-ventilated windowless pantry, well wrapped or covered by a bowl to keep off the flies.

Then the air raid sirens sounded with that ominous wail everyone came to know so well. We all sat transfixed, except father who drew the curtains and suggested we move under the stairs. It proved a false alarm, but created a profound impression on all of us.

James Lingard

* * *

As far as the war was concerned, there followed months when nothing seemed to happen which impinged on our safety and life did indeed carry on very much as normal. Father went to work as usual.

In the wider world, Poland suffered a Blitzkrieg and fell after no more than a month of heavy fighting, leaving Warsaw in ruins. The British navy saw immediate action and suffered some serious losses, but such is wartime propaganda that any publicity these received was couched in terms calculated not to alarm the population.

A relatively small British Expeditionary Force - far from well equipped - comprising much of the regular army went over to France, but for months France did not attack Germany and Germany did not attack France. Only in April 1940 did hostilities on that front commence in earnest.

As far as we were concerned in peaceful Petts Wood, some preparations were made to defend against bombing, which the population accepted with a degree of reluctance. Gas masks, carried in a cardboard box provided, were issued to protect the wearer from gas bombs - not that it was an offence to forget one's mask. The habit soon wore off, particularly away from London.

Children were supposed to have special Mickey Mouse masks, but mine was the standard hot smelly black rubber issue. My mother taught me how to put it on, but I hated it - breathing whilst wearing it was an effort. Fortunately, the German's never used gas against the British population.

A blackout was imposed from the 1st September 1939. All windows and doors had to be covered as darkness fell with heavy blackout curtains sufficient to prevent any glimmer of light escaping. Mother tried to argue that her floral curtains were sufficient, but the air raid wardens would have none of it and she ended up with plain black like everyone else.

More dangerous, street lights were dimmed - indeed switched off when the sirens sounded. Traffic lights and vehicle lights were hooded to deflect their beams downwards. Trees and lamp posts were painted with white stripes to make them more visible but road accidents dramatically increased. In my family, the result was that no-one except father went out after dark - bearable in the summer but dire on winter evenings, even though summer time was extended to last all year round and supplemented by the introduction of double summer time in May 1941.

The blackout seemed a good idea, but proved to be of limited value especially on moonlight nights - 'a bomber's moon'. The Thames remained visible from the air on most nights - a giveaway for London. Moreover strategic targets like railway marshalling yards, harbours and factories working through the night could not conceal their existence.

From the start of the war, petrol rationing came into force, followed by sugar, butter and bacon on the 8th January 1940 and all meat on the 11th March 1940. Rationing was gradually extended not only to many foods, but to clothes in June 1941 then coal, gas and electricity and even sweets. Poultry, potatoes, vegetables, fruit and fish were not rationed.

The amounts allowed were of necessity miserly - one fresh egg a week does not have much impact on one's waistline. In that respect, rationing had a beneficial effect on the population. It became lean and fit - no problem of overweight teenagers. Moreover, the shortages helped to mask the pressures of inflation. The price of clothes rose by 25% in the first six months after war was declared. Over the whole war, prices on average rose by a third - really heavy inflation came much later.

The Government did its best to guide the population on how to survive. School children were required, under the supervision of their teachers, to drink one third of a pint of milk provided for them at break time. A 'Dig for Victory' campaign was launched in October 1939 encouraging people to dig up their lawns and flower beds and plant vegetables. Potato Pete and Doctor Carrot proclaimed on posters that they made good soup. Dock leaf pudding is not unlike spinach if you are hungry enough. Pancakes made from flower and water are quite palatable.

A whole series of slogans sprang up: 'Careless Talk Costs Lives', 'Make Do and Mend', 'Coughs and Sneezes Spread Diseases' to name but a few. A campaign began to dig up and confiscate all iron railings. The metal was urgently required by the armaments industry. It took half a century for the country to recover from this!

Women were exhorted to mobilise themselves and fill the jobs vacated by men who went off to the war.

In particular, the Women's Land Army was formed in June 1939 to enable more food to be grown. If Germany believed it could starve us into submission by sinking the supply ships, Britain had better set about maximising the amount of food it could produce itself.

* * *

The big event for me in this period had to be the arrival of our Anderson shelter which father and a neighbour erected at the bottom of the garden in one weekend - father returning the favour the following weekend. To me, the shelter was rather like having a tent in the garden; to my parents, a constant reminder of the horrors expected to come. Mother swore she would never set foot in it - and as we shall see she never did.

I watched the erection of the shelter in fascination. First a pit three feet deep and measuring ten feet by five feet had to be dug - no mean feat on a warm summer day for a pair of office workers. All shelters had to be in place by the 11th June 1940 by Order under the Defence Regulations. My family like many others left it to the last minute - there had been no sign of enemy bombers.

The earth dug out had to be piled around the hole and later used to cover the finished structure to a depth of at least 15 inches - thirty inches on the sides and back. A pity the flat garden did not allow for effective drainage so that the bottom of the hole quickly became a puddle - not easy to avoid by torchlight in the dark.

Expert builders might have remedied the damp, but father was no expert.

The shelter itself comprised six corrugated curved iron sheets - three for each side - and two steel end pieces, all bolted together to form a hideaway six feet high in the centre of the arch, six feet six inches long and four feet six inches wide. The entrance also had the protection of an earthen blast wall, angled to deflect any blast over the roof.

Was an Anderson shelter out in the open any safer than a dry cupboard under the stairs, equipped with mattresses and cushions and reinforced by sandbags? Neither alternative was exactly healthy once the bombs started to fall and the ground to shake!

* * *

The seriousness of the war first hit me on the 7th June 1940 - my birthday. My parents had shielded me from all knowledge of the German invasion of Denmark and Norway in April of that year, securing for the enemy the continued supply of Swedish iron ore so vital to her war industry. This may have been intended by Hitler as a diversionary tactic masking the imminent attack on France, but it had one serious adverse consequence for the Germans. Their navy suffered serious loss, making it utterly unable to provide cover for a landing on the English coast.

Even the seriousness of the attack on France in the truly devastating blitzkrieg of May had not at first been appreciated by families back in Britain. Headlong retreat was presented as a series of tactical withdrawals. But when would the front hold?

Finally, the escape of 338,226 men, a major portion of the British Expeditionary Force, from Dunkirk (26th May to 4th June) was presented to the proud but stunned population as a victory. But they escaped without any of their heavy equipment and in many cases without weapons of any kind. The propaganda helped people to believe that the war could still be won, but in reality the Regular Army had become exhausted and acutely short of weapons. What chance would 450 or so semi-obsolete tanks stand against the Panzer Divisions which had swept some of our best troops out of France in a month?

The fall of France and the rout of allied forces had altered the whole shape of the war, and for the first time exposed Britain to heavy and sustained air attack. The Government prepared for invasion, formed the Home Guard from over a million and a quarter volunteers, and set about purchasing arms and ammunition of all kinds mainly from America and Canada.

Initially, the Home Guard had no military weapons - there were none to spare - but were taught to follow the example of Russian revolutionaries and make Molotov cocktails from bottles filled with petrol. Incredibly, women were not allowed to join despite having proved their worth in the armed forces.

Place names were removed from stations and the roads; signposts changed to send strangers in the wrong direction. Chaos reigned. Ringing church bells was forbidden; now they would be the signal that Germans had landed. If they did, civilians were instructed to stay put - not clog the roads as refugees had done in France.

Where would the Germans land - by parachute or by sea? Perhaps in small numbers at first - we knew they were short of landing craft. Obstacles were placed in fields to obstruct gliders. The whole country went on alert. Churchill resolved not to spread his troops too thin as the French had done; battle groups were placed in strategic locations.

* * *

The 7th June dawned bright and sunny and mother and I with two other young families were invited to spend the afternoon in the garden of a near neighbour who worked with father. This boasted a small plunge pool, too small to swim in but ideal for young children to splash about and keep cool, whilst our mothers sat and chatted in the shade of a nearby apple tree.

My mother went indoors to prepare some sandwiches - rationing precluded anything too elaborate. Suddenly one of the others burst into tears and began to sob uncontrollably. 'What will happen to little Chrissie and me when the Germans invade,' she wailed. 'I don't know what to do.' Her friends stared at her in horror.

What would it be like to live under German masters? There were horrific rumours of how Belgian women were being abused. They tried to comfort her without much conviction or success. 'She's jewish,' I heard one of them whisper, without understanding the significance of the comment.

'How dare you suggest such a thing as invasion in front of the children,' mother exploded when she returned. 'The Germans invade indeed. That's defeatist talk, I won't have it.' Defeatist talk had been made an offence by the Defence Regulations. Britain had ceased to be the free and easy country of pre-war days. We were at war and had better get used to the idea.

I had to admire her stoicism. But the calm bliss of the suburban tea party was shattered. Petts Wood would never be the same for me again. The party broke up - mother and I were left to eat our own sandwiches.

* * *

Chapter 3

My First Bomb

> '- - we shall not flag or fail. We shall go on to the end. We shall fight in France, we shall fight in the seas and oceans, we shall fight with growing confidence and strength in the air; we shall defend our Island, whatever the cost may be. We shall fight on the beaches, we shall fight on the landing-grounds, we shall fight in the fields and in the streets, we shall fight in the hills; we shall never surrender -' (Winston Churchill 4th June 1940)

One weekend, a few days after my birthday, father suggested we have a picnic tea in the woods a mile or so from home. We found a delightful shady open space amongst the silver birch trees, hidden from the path by a clump of rhododendron bushes, and spread out a rug to bask in the sunshine. Mother remarked how near to London we were, yet listening to birdsong on a glorious afternoon as if in the heart of the countryside.

As we began to pack up, father told us this might be our last picnic in Petts Wood. The war situation had worsened dramatically. Italy had declared war on us on the 10th June and France had surrendered on the 17th. London was now within range of enemy bombers and we stood alone. Much of our army had been rescued from Dunkirk, but their equipment was lost and would take months to replace.

He had thought of volunteering for the army, but had been asked to stay on at the bank for a few weeks.

It was a war priority to preserve the banking system and to that end Lloyds head office was to be split up and moved out of London. His team was moving a section to Bournemouth, starting as soon as possible, and he suggested we move there with him. 'You might even get a summer holiday after all!'

Mother beamed. The weather was perfect; the summer of 1940 was truly gloriously sunny - just as the winter which followed turned out to be one of the coldest on record. We all needed a holiday - the whole country. The realisation that we were all but defenceless gave everyone the horrors, but a grim determination to struggle on to the end.

Then suddenly and quite unexpectedly, the air raid warning sounded - not the short test bursts of siren we were accustomed to but a prolonged undulating wail, taken up by another siren in the distance and then a third. What to do caught out there in the open - not a shelter in sight?

Father pointed to a tiny dell, not twenty yards away. 'Quick. Grab your gas masks; keep under the trees; we'll make for that.' He ushered us into a hollow and made us lie flat. Bushes sheltered us on three sides, the fourth had no cover. 'Never mind. Can't be helped, but we're hardly a prime target.'

Silence. Minutes passed. Could it be a false alarm? No way of knowing. We fingered our gas masks nervously, but refrained from putting them on.

Then the splutter of a single low flying aircraft. We could see it quite clearly slowly hauling itself over the hill to our left and heading across our little patch of woodland towards Petts Wood and the south coast beyond. The black crosses on its wings and fuselage and the swastika on its tail proclaimed it to be enemy.

It might have struck terror into me, but all was plainly not well with the intruder. Black smoke trailed from one of its twin engines, and I had considerable doubt about whether the pilot would climb the ridge ahead. Somehow he did, hugging the contours of the land. Up above, the sun glinted on the wings of a Spitfire watching over its damaged adversary.

'Keep very still,' father commanded. 'That plane's finished. The men inside are desperate. They could do anything. It's a Messerschmitt 110 - a fighter bomber probing our air defences. We don't know whether it's dropped its bomb load or not.'

It had not, but as he spoke the pilot jettisoned his last remaining bomb in a final attempt to gain height. We heard the explosion in the general direction of home. Mother and I froze - held our breath as though the Germans might hear us. But the planes were gone and the loud high pitched whine of the all clear quickly followed.

Time to collect our things and go home - the mood for basking in the sun had evaporated. The wood had become a hostile environment, almost a battle-ground where men fought and died - or so it seemed to me.

Once we reached the main road, mother brightened: 'We're going on holiday. Bournemouth. The sea. Fresh air. That's much better than these rows and rows of houses, all so similar in design.'

But when we came to our street, we found it cordoned off and two policemen barring our way. 'Sorry, sir. You'll have to go round. There's been a

Britain at War 1939 to 1945

bomb. The air raid wardens are still combing the area for bodies. Three people are missing.'

Father protested that we lived in the road and needed to go home. 'Try the church hall down there. They'll give you a cup of tea, and you'll find your neighbours who'll tell you all about it.'

We had no option and followed his directions with a sense of growing curiosity and excitement. Mother was never one to make a grand entrance, preferring to slip into a room unobtrusively. This time she was greeted by a collective gasp, emphasised by one friend of ours who dropped her cup and slumped to the floor.

'It's them. It is, isn't it? I'm not dreaming, am I? We were told you'd been blown to bits. Are you alright?

A serious looking warden interposed himself. 'Your full names and address please. Come and sit at that table in the corner over there.' He ushered us over to the make-do privacy of his little domain. 'You've put a lot of people to a lot of trouble. Why didn't you report in half an hour ago when the all clear sounded?'

His attitude annoyed father who told him where we had been. 'In the woods; in an air raid. That's no way to take care of your - -.' He stopped in mid-sentence, swallowed and flushed. 'I'm sorry, so sorry. I was about to say you should have been in your shelter. But the shelter received a direct hit. There's no trace of it. Just a huge crater. You'd all have been blown to smithereens. We thought you had. You've had a lucky escape. Excuse me whilst I call off the search.'

I looked at mother who had turned very pale and gripped father's hand. 'Would we have been in that shelter? Please tell me we wouldn't. I never did like it. What a place to die.' and she sobbed.

Father looked very serious. 'I don't know, but clearly we weren't meant to die. Not this time anyway. It's probably best if you stay here whilst I see if I can arrange somewhere for tonight. I'll see what sort of state the house is in and rescue what I can of our things. Feel sorry for the wretched landlord. The sooner we're out the better.'

Mother joined her friends in the hall; to hugs and kisses and tears. The bomb could have fallen on any of them and they knew it. We all had a very emotional evening. Even more so when father returned in a car with two of his colleagues from work and announced we were moving to Chislehurst immediately. The bomb had blown in all the windows in the back of the house - slivers of razor sharp glass everywhere - and half the roof had gone.

'The house is much too dangerous even to look round. I have our valuables and what we really need. The wardens are boarding it up. We've all been bloody lucky there are no casualties. The war is taking us away from Petts Wood. Good luck to all of you. I'm sorry but this has to be goodbye.'

I cannot remember the precise words spoken, but the bomb was real enough and the scenario typical for those lucky enough not to have been at home when the Nazis called.

* * *

CHAPTER 4

Battle Of Britain

> '- - Never in the field of human conflict was so much owed by so many to so few.' (Winston Churchill on the Battle of Britain September 1940)

Plans for the German invasion of Britain required the Luftwaffe to establish complete mastery of the air over the Channel and South-east England. Once their forces had captured the airfields of Northern France, their numerical operational superiority in the air made this seem almost inevitable to Hitler. At the start of the battle, apart from a 1,000 or so bombers and 350 Stuka dive bombers, the Germans could call on 933 fighters - many of which were Messerschmitt 109s - and in addition 375 Messerschmitt 110 fighter bombers.

Against them the British had 19 squadrons of Spitfires and 38 squadrons of Hurricanes making between 600 and 700 aircraft available to fight at any one time throughout the battle. British aircraft production had reached the point where new machines almost exactly equalled losses - an average of 62 Hurricanes and 33 Spitfires each week throughout the Battle of Britain. German industry only produced half that number of fighters. Experienced pilots were another matter, but many of those shot down were able to parachute to safety. 481 were killed or taken prisoner by the enemy.

The British also had the advantage of a secret weapon whose significance the Germans did not appreciate. We had in place along the south coast an effective radar system with a range of eighty miles - enough warning to get the fighters in the air. It also estimated the height of the incoming aircraft, but this aspect proved to be less reliable.

The German strategy from the 10th July to the 18th August 1940 was to harry convoys in the Channel and the south coast ports to draw our fighters into battle and then destroy them. They made a special effort in the week ending 17th August shooting down no less than 134 British fighters, though they believed their tally was materially greater and were unaware of the number of replacement planes entering service. On the other hand, the Germans lost 261 aircraft according to their own records (which may have been mollified to pacify Hitler) - the RAF claimed 496.

15th August saw the heaviest fighting of the battle; all available British aircraft took part. In addition to major attacks on south east England, the Germans launched 100 heavy bombers escorted by 40 Me110 fighter bombers against Tyneside - believing it to be a soft target without fighter cover. They were detected before reaching the coast and met by elements of seven experienced British fighter squadrons which had been sent to the area to rest and regroup. Thirty German aircraft were shot down as they broke formation and fled, for a British loss of two pilots injured.

The Tyneside raid demonstrated that the Me110 was no match for either Hurricanes or Spitfires. It was too slow and lacked maneuverability - though it subsequently demonstrated its value as a night fighter. Equally, the dive bombers, whilst deadly as they screamed down on their targets, became sitting ducks for the fighters as they pulled out of the dive.

The Me109 was a more deadly foe, but limited in range and therefore in the time it could spend over Britain. It could out dive the Spitfires in service at the time, but lacked their maneuverability and the fire power of eight wing-mounted 0.303 machine guns. RAF tactics, when given the choice, was for Spitfires to attack the Messerschmitts, whilst Hurricanes took on the bombers.

The low point of the battle for the British came in the fortnight commencing 24th August, when 466 of our fighters were destroyed or seriously damaged with the loss of 231 pilots. On that day, Manston airfield was totally destroyed and never became operational again. True the Germans lost 380 planes and that over 250 new fighters rolled off the British production lines, but such a high rate of attrition could not have been maintained for long. Miraculously, Hitler believed that the RAF had been smashed beyond recovery and, as a reprisal for an RAF raid on Berlin, ordered his bombers to attack London instead of the fighter bases - his first major strategic error of the war.

London suffered heavily, particularly over the following ten days when the Luftwaffe made a final effort to establish supremacy and enable an invasion to be launched. In so doing, they suffered heavy losses - in excess of 600 aircraft in five weeks - double the British losses in the period.

Even worse for Goering, on the night of 15th September, a heavy raid on London met an even stronger force of British fighters. 34 of the attacking bombers were shot down and a further 20 damaged. Then, British bombers counter-attacked and inflicted crippling damage on the invasion barges which the Germans had assembled. The invasion of Britain had to be postponed indefinitely.

The Germans switched to night raids where our fighters were much less effective, but the Thames - glinting in the moonlight - betrayed London and it suffered just as heavily as before. For fifty seven consecutive nights from the 7th September 1940, London shook under the pounding of high explosives and burned in fire storms which took decades to repair. Roughly fifty thousand people died in the blitz.

The air raid shelters - and in London the underground - saved many lives. However, two and a quarter million people were made homeless - many more than the Authorities had anticipated. They needed food, clothing and shelter immediately, but the rescue services quickly became overwhelmed. That was part of the horror of the blitz - thousands lost everything they had including much loved relatives. Fortunately, voluntary services such as the Canadian Red Cross stepped in to help. Local Authorities only became empowered to requisition empty properties in April 1941.

The Germans then set about attempting to destroy Britain's war production. The centre of Coventry was destroyed on 14th November 1940, followed by Birmingham the next week and Liverpool at the end of the month. Surprisingly, machine tools in the factories were little damaged and production quickly resumed.

Bombing switched to ports around the country, including Manchester with its ship canal just before Christmas, then back to London on 29th December 1940 where the City of London suffered an awesome fire storm which burned for days. Somehow, St Paul's Cathedral survived.

* * *

As for my family, we arrived in Bournemouth towards the end of June to find the resort still in holiday mode. Most families had decided to stay at home in the emergency, but our home had been bombed. The town was generally considered to be a safe refuge of no strategic importance. How could we know of Hitler's plan to entice Britain's fighters into the air by bombing the south coast? In any case, there had to be more important targets.

Father found us a pleasant hotel about a mile from the town centre - a short walk from the building his bank had selected for a division of its head office. We all shared a room facing away from the sea. He went off to work each morning and mother and I walked down to sun ourselves on the beach in the company of a fair number of like minded holidaymakers. The arrangement was of necessity temporary but nobody knew where father would be sent next.

One particular morning towards the middle of July, we arrived a little later than usual to find the beach quite crowded with mothers and young children below school age. The calm sea looked blue and inviting so we went for a paddle before settling down to build a sandcastle against the incoming tide. The ripples began to wash it away; I struggled to shore it up.

A rustle of excitement from a group nearby caused me to look up. Mother lay half asleep in some shade nearby - it could not be important. But one of them kept pointing out to sea. I looked, but the sun in my eyes soon had me back to the ruins of the sandcastle.

'It's coming this way.' I looked again. Out on the horizon, a tiny speck flew very low above the surface of the sea, laboriously making its way directly towards us. Everyone settled down to watch the mystery - a single seater aircraft flying slowly below the height of the cliffs. What was it doing? Was it looking for something floating in the sea? A mine perhaps.

Nearer and nearer. Two hundred yards - one hundred yards. A gasp: 'It can't be. The siren hasn't gone.' A woman behind me screamed. I turned to look and all the adults on the beach threw themselves flat, face down on the sand. Astonishing!

I looked up at the plane, now thirty yards away and no more than forty feet above the sea. The pilot was clearly visible in a black uniform and he grinned broadly at the panic below him. I waved happily; he waved back and flew on over my head.

Then I saw for the first time the black cross on the side of the tiny plane and the small swastika on its tail. But this aircraft looked so harmless, too small to carry bombs and no sign of any weapon.

A man's voice yelled: 'Grab that child. He's signaling to the enemy.' I looked up to see an angry police sergeant heading towards me.

Mother launched herself out of nowhere and flattened me. 'He's only a child. He doesn't know anything about the war. We're only here because our house was bombed.' It took her a good five minutes to satisfy the policeman of my innocence and the people around shrank away from us. She marched me firmly back to the hotel and made me promise never again to waive at any Germans. 'That's the last time we go to that particular beach, but I expect we'll find another one.'

That evening, she told father. He looked grave. 'That must have been a spotter plane taking photographs, but why here.'

'Why did no one shoot it down? It was so low, they could hardly have missed.'

'Nobody was on guard. Nobody expected it. This could be serious. And you young man, next time you keep your head down like everyone else.'

* * *

Two nights later, we learned the reason for the spotter plane. My parents had just said goodnight to me when the sirens sounded the alarm. We all looked at one another and reached for the gas masks. Could it be a false alarm? A hotel porter made his way down the corridor banging on each door and shouting: 'Air raid. Everyone down the staircase and into the cellar. Quick as you can.'

Father shook his head. 'No. I'm not leaving this room. Damned uncomfortable spending the night in a cellar crowded with people shivering with fear. Anyway, remember the Anderson shelter I put up. If we'd used that, we'd have been done for.'

Mother pleaded with him to go. 'Think of the child.'

'I am. My view is that if a bomb has your name on it, you're dead whatever you do; if it doesn't, you're OK.' He stuck to this belief in predestination right through the London blitz and his army service. In time of real danger, it can be a great comfort to know that your fate is decided by God whatever you do.

Still no sign of enemy attack. Mother began to relax and I went back to bed. Then we heard the first explosions - a good way off - no need to panic, but time to pray. A pause. Then a second set of explosions decidedly louder - nearer this time. Things were getting exciting. I pulled the bedclothes over my head.

The third set was close - close enough not only to rattle the windows but to shake the building. Father put his hand on my shoulder. 'Roll under the bed if it helps. We won't mind.' I shook my head - but mother did shelter under her bed. Father's doctrine of predestination is no good unless you really believe in it.

No sooner had the rumble of the explosions died away than we heard the loud drone of dozens of low flying aircraft coming straight at us. No sign of any fighters intercepting them. No ack ack guns. We were on our own, just us and the bombers overhead. The moment of truth.

They totally ignored us - just flew on and turned over the sea back to France without a shot being fired at them as far as we could tell. Bournemouth had indeed been a soft target. It had ceased to be a comfortable refuge. Would they load up with more bombs and come straight back? None of us slept much that night, though father insisted we stay in bed and tried to sleep.

I don't know what effect air raids had on other children, but that one had a peculiar impact on me. Mother had spent the previous afternoon teaching me how to read out of an illustrated book of fairy stories. One had a full page coloured picture depicting three witches circling over a small hamlet on broomsticks, each with a black cat sitting behind her. I had a nightmare that it was those witches which had caused the explosions around me.

Mother was not amused. But then she had her own problems. Father explained to us over breakfast that he had been summoned back to London. Some branches of the bank had been hit by bombs. His team was needed to go in and save what could be saved. He would do this until the bombing eased and then join the army. He preferred to face the enemy with a gun in his hand and hit back. We could not go with him to London. It would be time to say goodbye that evening.

They discussed what to do and decided she and I should go and live with grandfather in Yorkshire. We both qualified as evacuees as I had not yet started school but would need to do so in September. Bournemouth had now joined London and the other south coast towns as potential targets from which the Government strongly recommended all children to be evacuated.

In this period of great sadness, mother tried to cheer me up by a last visit to our favourite beach. Not a good idea. We arrived at the cliff top to find access to the sea was prohibited. Down below, we could see perhaps a thousand soldiers constructing tank traps, laying mines and unrolling miles of barbed wire. Lorries towing guns were arriving in convoys. Bournemouth had woken up to its new position in the front line. If the Germans returned, they would not find it a soft target next time.

This was no place for children. No more beach holiday. Time to move on.

* * *

CHAPTER 5

On The Move

> '- - The present system of air-raid warnings was designed to cope with occasional large mass raids - - not with waves coming over several times a day, and still less with sporadic bombers roaming about at night. We cannot allow large parts of the country to be immobilised for hours every day and to be distracted every night.' (Winston Churchill to Home Secretary 1st September 1940)

In the period 7th September to 3rd November 1940, an average of 200 German bombers attacked London every night – supplemented by constant small daytime raids to harry the population. Father endured that experience throughout, and mother – knowing his aversion to air-raid shelters – lived in permanent fear that she would never see him again. In fact, like thousands of others, he spent most nights in an underground station – relatively safe, but thoroughly uncomfortable.

As for mother and me, we were still stuck in Bournemouth but determined to join grandfather in the West Riding of Yorkshire when it became possible. But how? Father made it very clear that London had to be avoided at all costs. Petrol rationing made travel by car impossible. Coaches – or charabancs as they were called – existed, but were requisitioned to move troops to strategic positions in the event of invasion.

James Lingard

That left the railway using a west coast route to Manchester, where grandfather could pick us up by car. He regularly visited the city on business – his clothing factory having been converted to manufacture military uniforms. But travel by train proved no easy matter even for evacuees, the majority of whom had been evacuated the previous year. Not many citizens of Bournemouth wanted to go to our destination, especially as Manchester was an even greater potential target for enemy bombers. Mother herself delayed the journey until close to Christmas.

Even before sections of the system were vested in the War Department, the principal priority of the railways had to be the transport of troops and military supplies to the vulnerable south coast. America sold us considerable quantities of arms to replace those lost at Dunkirk and these tended to be landed at Liverpool or Manchester.

The threat of imminent invasion also led to the use of armed trains, heavy naval guns mounted on flat carriages. One of these, an eighteen inch monster, had a range of over twelve miles and fired shells six feet long.

No wonder the railways became a strategic target for sporadic bombers or even enemy fighters low on fuel and returning to France with ammunition to spare. No hope of trains running to timetable – too dangerous to publicise their itinerary. Wait patiently, and take your chance when it comes.

Eventually, we boarded a succession of trains which crawled along to our destination – frequently diverted into sidings or around loops in order to give way to high priority military traffic. The food we took with us did not last and we were compelled to rely on railway buffets. These sold stale sandwiches and rock hard buns, washed down in my case with water and in mother's with a substance euphemistically called tea, but bearing little resemblance to any now on sale.

On arriving at Crewe, we learned that Manchester had been heavily bombed the night before and that the area around Victoria station was still ablaze. All services to Manchester were suspended until further notice. Mother telephoned grandfather who told her to stay put for two days and then try again. Meanwhile, he would remain in Hebden Bridge.

* * *

When we eventually arrived at a devastated Victoria station, the square outside the entrance still smoldered with an all pervasive smell of burning. Fire engines, police and air-raid wardens swarmed everywhere, and mother and I were viewed with incredulity. What were we doing in a hell like this? Surely we had more sense than to go sightseeing – there could be unexploded bombs.

Grandfather found us and apologized that he had left the car some distance away – all the roads were closed. However, he had succeeded in booking us into lunch at the Victoria Hotel, one of the best in Manchester. How wrong he was to regard this as an achievement. The restaurant, like the hotel, proved to be virtually empty. The bombing had been so devastating that no one, including mother, wished to remain anywhere near. The sound of collapsing buildings being torn down does not improve the appetite.

We must hurry or the restaurant will stop serving, he kept saying. Mother protested that she was in no fit state to patronise such a place, but nowhere else in the vicinity was open and we were ravenous.

One of the quirks of rationing permitted food to be served in restaurants, but Government regulations imposed a maximum price of five shillings per person – twenty five pence in modern money, though inflation has greatly devalued the currency of that time. The Victoria continued to produce relatively exotic meals, but the slices of melon were cut wafer thin. Never having eaten melon before, I only discovered the abnormality of this after the war.

* * *

Hebden Bridge had seen little of the war, some men had joined the armed forces, occasionally the sirens sounded but enemy bombers had more worthwhile targets in neighbouring towns. We climbed the steep hill to grandfather's house and mother received something of a heroine's welcome. However, she and I were to sleep in the attic and the stairs to that were steep and inconvenient.

Mother acknowledged that she could play the piano and was promptly ushered into the front room to demonstrate. But what to play? Handel unrehearsed she dismissed as too difficult – a decision sympathetically received. 'We don't mind. Play something you know.' She did. A piece of Boogie-Woogie learned in the

United States and played fast and competently. Mother was not going to demean herself to grandfather's puritanical regime.

They gave us tea, literally home-made bread and jam and a cup of tea for the adults – milk for me. Milk delivered in churns direct from the local farms seemed to be plentiful in the area throughout the war. After tea, mother expressed herself to be exhausted and suggested a bath then bed.

'Sorry, no hot water for a bath. There will be in the morning.' Life in Yorkshire was more primitive than in Petts Wood or Bournemouth, but at least we felt safe – or did we?

'Do you have an air-raid shelter?' mother asked as she turned to go upstairs. They showed her the door to the cellar.

The problems soon emerged, as they did for many evacuees. The house was really too small for all five of us. In particular, the bathroom contained the only toilet and grandmother insisted on the front room remaining in pristine condition in case unexpected visitors called. Our stay could only be temporary – over the Christmas holidays.

Father telephoned from London to tell us that the bank no longer needed him. He had volunteered to join the army. This might be the last we heard from him for some time, particularly if he got posted overseas. 'I'll miss you desperately, but if you could see what they've done to London, you'd understand.'

He added that he had bought a disused farm cottage in Pecket Well – a small hamlet in the Pennines overlooking Hebden Bridge. Grandfather was arranging for workmen to replace the rotten timber floor with concrete and generally to make the place habitable. He was careful not to suggest any degree of comfort, much less luxury.

The call distressed mother, indeed all of us. She really might lose him and be stranded with me in a tiny village where she knew nobody. Grandmother did her best to reassure us, but stopped short of begging us not to leave.

* * *

Pecket Well straddles the road from Hebden Bridge to Keighley at the point where it emerges from the steep wooded slopes to run just below the crest of the hill. Incongruously, it boasts a small mill, though no one I met knew quite what this manufactured. Could it have been some vital part for the Hurricane fighter? We were not allowed near.

More conventionally, it had a pub, a general store / sub-post office, a village policeman and a small school with two class rooms. Nothing more – no church or chapel – but hill farm after farm stretching all the way to the moors in the distance.

We were close to Bronte country and the farms reminded mother of Wuthering Heights – creepy on a dark night. The village had no street lights to be blacked out! Worse, the electricity was carried on telegraph poles. When the wind got up, it howled through the wires like a wailing banshee. We did not go out after dark except to the toilet in a hut in the garden – and that was exciting, poor mother.

Our cottage stood down a short lane on the edge of the village nearest to the moors. It had belonged to the farm close-by. Its tiny garden backed on to the farm yard and the smell of manure could be overpowering when the wind blew from the south. The accommodation comprised a small living room heated by a log fire, one bedroom and a minute kitchen. No bathroom – just a tin bath to use in front of the fire – but we did have electricity (if no power cut intervened) and running water from the reservoir nearby.

One problem we never overcame. The structure, built of granite and concrete, had no damp course. It rains a lot in Yorkshire and the winters are biting cold. Our cottage seemed to suck in the damp; everything in it became damp and that means cold. The pipes froze that winter, and a deep snow drift cut us off from the rest of the village.

Fortunately, we did dig our way through to the farmhouse. The farmer helped with logs, eggs and milk in return for mother helping part time in the farm kitchen. Once I started school, she had to register for war work and help in the post office as well as the farm. She struggled on without complaining, but with no form of leisure activity. Life was work, and she worked hard, as did many others in the same position.

* * *

CHAPTER 6

Village Life

> '- - Without allowing the women of Britain to enter the struggle as they desire to do, we should fail utterly to bear our fair share of the burden which France and Britain have jointly assumed. (Winston Churchill speaking at Manchester 27th January 1940).

The Women's Land Army was formed before the war in June 1939 in a desperate attempt to produce more home grown food by cultivating every available square inch of fertile ground. Food production gradually increased by 90%, but this was still less than half the food needed to feed the population. A 'Dig for Victory' campaign urged people to dig up their lawns and flower beds and plant vegetables instead.

Much of the food imported came in dehydrated form to save space on the ships which had to run the gauntlet of German U-Boats. Dried bananas became a favourite of mine, to the point that after the war I preferred them to fresh ones. This shocked a greengrocer who called me a poor deprived child. Dried potatoes and dried eggs were nutritious, but horrible.

Mother never became a 'Land Girl' but we met them at harvest time. Indeed, the whole village (including me) was mobilised and given implements to cut corn growing in fields too steep for agricultural machinery. I well remember one hot day being sent home from school and instructed how to use a small curved blade about a foot long, whilst the men carved great swathes in the corn with two handed scythes. My task entailed following them at a safe distance and cutting any tufts they might have missed. The cut corn was then forked onto a horse drawn cart and taken to a threshing machine in the farm yard.

How did school differ from today? For a start, children made their own way to school unaccompanied - mothers of school age children had to work and petrol rationing made it impractical to drive to school. In my case, this entailed a walk of perhaps half a mile from one end of the village to the other. Not entirely risk free, but then life in wartime could never be that. On one occasion, I was bitten by one of the village dogs and the teacher enquired about my bloodstained appearance. By the time school ended, the dog had been caught and shot.

Like most evacuees, I endured life in a closed community, a stranger with a different accent who had been imposed on the others by an accident of war. Naturally, an attempt was made to bully me, but father had always impressed upon me how to punch. I did, with results which soon deterred further aggression against me.

After a while, mother and I came to be accepted. Mother had been born and bred in Halifax - not many miles away. Moreover, our cottage was every bit as cold and damp as the others, and our lifestyle no better than theirs. Indeed, being down a lane on the edge of the village, we were even more isolated than most.

The village boys showed me hideaways in the woods and short cuts through the fields. We even

James Lingard

braved the local bull field together. The contours of the hill prevented the whole field being visible from the style which gave entry, and more than once we had to run for it when the bull came thundering over the ridge.

I had one big advantage over the other children - mother taught me how to read, write and do simple sums before I even started school. However, my writing was and is appalling. The teacher constantly complained that she could not read it. One day she offered a prize for the neatest copy of a short text - a pencil sold to raise funds for the French who had escaped to Britain. It had some writing in French and a tricolor at the end. I wanted that pencil, even though my conception of liberty equality and fraternity at that time was negligible. I really concentrated on the task in hand and produced immaculate copper plate to her utter astonishment.

At school, we were all given a dark blue card issued by the RAF on which were the black silhouettes of eight aircraft; four British and four German. If we saw any German planes, we were to count how many of each type and inform the nearest adult who should immediately tell the police. A little later, the village from its vantage point near the crest of the hill did see its first German bombers lumbering noisily and painfully slowly across the skyline. But the local policeman made it very clear in unmistakable and unprintable terms that he did not need our assistance in counting them!

After school, mother allowed me to listen to the radio - the wireless as it was then called. Children's Hour - in practice never more than half an hour at this period - and in particular Toy town became my firm favourite. Mother liked Music While You Work, jaunty popular music such as 'Run, Rabbit, Run' played at a fast tempo to speed up production in the factories.

The news was barred to me, though mother would listen to it later. Imagine my horror on the rare occasions Children's Hour had to be cancelled to make way for an extended news bulletin -invariably at that period news full of one disaster after another.

* * *

What was happening in the outside world in late 1940, early 1941? This was the low point in the war for the British, despite the propaganda attempts to make every withdrawal 'tactical' and our losses allegedly less than those of the enemy.

We had hoped that when France fell, its navy would escape to British ports and continue the fight. Unfortunately, major units remained at their base in Toulon and under the Vichy Government maintained hostile neutrality. On the 25th September 1940, Vichy forces reinforced from Toulon repulsed free French troops commanded by General De Gaulle when he tried to liberate Dakar in West Africa. Supporting British warships suffered some damage and casualties, as did the French. Had our former friends suddenly turned against us?

There were some redeeming features in the grand scale of things. The RAF had decisively established its superiority over the enemy during the daytime in British airspace. Unfortunately, our night fighters were less effective and the Germans switched their bombing to hours of darkness. One of the heaviest raids on London occurred as late as the 10th May 1941 when in excess of three thousand people were killed.

This did not feel like victory in the air to those suffering the bombing, but in fact the RAF had done enough to lift the threat of invasion. Then again, night time bombing could smash cities, but not pinpoint the factories vital to our war effort. These worked night and day pouring out aircraft, tanks and munitions. Britain was steadily rearming after Dunkirk, where the retreating troops had been forced to abandon all their heavy guns and equipment. Once again, we had a strong army, thanks in part to the import of arms from America. The USA still remained officially neutral, but shipped over to us much needed food and military supplies.

We even felt strong enough to launch some offensive actions, particularly against the Italians who were threatening to wrest control of the Mediterranean from us. On the 11th November 1940, our Mediterranean fleet attacked the Italian navy massing in Taranto and successfully torpedoed three battleships and inflicted heavy damage on the dockyard. Three nights later, the Luftwaffe countered any uplift in British morale by smashing Coventry with over one thousand civilian casualties. The RAF retaliated by bombing Hamburg. Nobody was safe.

On the 9th December 1940, the 7th Armoured Division drove back the numerically superior Italian divisions which were threatening Egypt, capturing Tobruk on the 22nd January 1941. Allied successes in the desert inflicted heavy losses on the Italians. However, once Hitler finally accepted that his tanks could not cross the Channel and attack Britain, he intervened decisively in support of the Italians.

Rommel and his Panzers first struck in the desert on 24th March 1941. A month later, they had driven the Allies all the way back to Egypt. April proved to be a month of disasters for us. Yugoslavia surrendered to the Germans on the 17th; and Greece, which had initially defended itself successfully against the Italians, fell on the 21st after a three week German blitzkrieg.

We still had no effective answer to the German might. Hitler's bombers continued to harass us and he tried his utmost to starve us into submission. In the period May to December 1940, the enemy sank 745 merchant vessels with a gross tonnage of over three million tons. On17th to 19th October 1940, German U-boats sank 33 ships, twenty of which were in one convoy they succeeded in ambushing.

We could not take losses like that for long. The Americans helped. Some of their own ships had been lost and this spurred them into lending us fifty of their older destroyers, primarily for convoy escort duties. These vessels first went into action in March 1941. But in the following months heavy losses continued, reaching a peak in November 1942. Food rations had to be reduced in 1941 and in April that year the media were forbidden to report on sinkings.

Britain and her Commonwealth tried desperately to save Crete as a Mediterranean base, but it fell to German paratroops in May 1941 after fierce fighting. This was one of the mistakes of the war, because it enabled the Germans to reinforce Rommel's crack Panzer Divisions in North Africa. We failed to supply our troops with fighter aircraft, tanks or even sufficient ammunition. Some were evacuated, but thousands were abandoned and imprisoned by the Germans.

May 1941 proved to be the low point in the war for Britain. Conditions then were grim indeed. The armed forces needed more men, but so did the munitions industry. Under the Essential Work Order of March 1941, one and a half million women were conscripted into doing war work to release more men to fight. By January 1943, ten million women had registered for war work. They took jobs previously the preserve of men and found that they could do them - but they received and still receive less pay.

We could not foresee that our enemies would soon make catastrophic miscalculations of their own, and that powerful forces would soon join us in our struggle for survival.

* * *

CHAPTER 7

Isle Of Man

> '- - In the spring, our U-boat war will begin at sea, and they will notice that we have not been sleeping. And the Air Force will play its part, and the entire armed forces will force a decision by hook or by crook.' (Hitler speaking in Berlin 30th January 1941).

In the first quarter of 1941, the Germans built ten new U-boats a month, a total rapidly increased to eighteen a month. In addition, the Focke-Wulf long range bomber began to fly sorties around the British Isles from Brest to Norway reporting the position of any allied convoys they sighted to the submarine wolf packs. Our losses increased dramatically. And in early February, the battle cruisers Scharnhorst and Gneisenau slipped past the British Home Fleet in fog and sank or captured twenty two merchant ships in the Atlantic.

These horrendous statistics were kept secret. How could mother and I have known? One evening in May, grandfather paid us a surprise visit. My father had telephoned him at work that afternoon - a momentous event which had never happened before since dad had joined the army. Mother went pale, something terrible must have happened.

No. The simple message had been that father had a week's leave, but he had been ordered to spend it in the Isle of Man. He had invited mother and me - but not grandfather - to take the Saturday morning ferry from Liverpool to Douglas and join him.

Grandfather advised against. Liverpool docks had become a prime target for German bombers. Merseyside had been bombed seven nights in a row at the beginning of the month, killing 1,900 people and the whole area was a disaster zone. True the raids had all been at night, but such a journey was beset with obvious danger, if indeed it proved possible for civilians to travel to the Island.

Mother quickly recovered her composure. 'We're going,' she exclaimed defiantly. 'If he wants us there, that's it. We're going. It may be the last time I ever see him.'

She quickly packed a few clothes and bundled me into grandfather's car. We would spend the night at his house and then see if trains were running to Manchester and from there to Liverpool.

* * *

The journey to Liverpool proved surprisingly easy. For once Manchester and the railways seemed to be functioning normally - well as near to normal as they ever did in wartime. We had made an early start and arrived at the docks around 10.30am.

Chaos. Where did the ferry depart? The normal booking office had been bombed. People seemed most reluctant to help - but the location of the ferry office could hardly be a state secret - could it?

In desperation, mother presented us at the police station and explained the situation. Did we have a pass? No. If father was in the army, did we have a letter or telegram from him? No. Then she had a flash of inspiration: 'My husband will have all the necessary papers. He'll be waiting for us by the ferry, but I can't find the ferry.'

This seemed to solve the sergeant's dilemma. 'Trouble is there may not be a ferry today. There are warnings of severe gales. They won't risk it if there's a storm.'

Mother was on the verge of tears. There had to be a ferry and we had to be on it. The sergeant gave us directions to the pier where the ferry normally docked and we hastened there as fast as we could. And there she was, a real old bucket of a ferry dating from the days of the Titanic and rather the worse for wear.

No sign of father; no message from him; no papers. The crew chose to be helpful. 'Are you sure you really want to sail today in the teeth of a gale to the prison island? It's no holiday resort these days you know.'

Mother did not know, but chose to keep that to herself. 'My husband's in the army. He's sent for us. I must see him.'

They took us on board, but looked at us as if we were off our heads. 'We won't be sailing until the wind abates, but we'll be the first ferry to leave.' No one said anything about being the first to arrive.

* * *

The Captain decided it would be safer to sail sooner rather than later, certainly before dark when the bombing started. He announced that it would be a rough trip and if anyone wanted to get off, they were welcome to do so. Mother shook her head. We were going - no argument.

She and I stood by the rail on the bow of the ferry watching the sailors cast off - and we were away. Mother's mood brightened perceptively, we really were going after all. Six years earlier, she had sailed from Liverpool in a P&O liner to New York on her honeymoon. The memories came flooding back as she pointed out the landmarks as they came into view. Many of the buildings had been destroyed or damaged, but she pointed out the huge pier at which the liner had been berthed. Our battered old ferry must have been a poor substitute, but I could tell from her excited tone that in her imagination she relived one of the great events of her life.

As we approached the open sea, one of the sailors handed us life jackets. 'Captain's orders ma'am. All passengers must wear life jackets. It's going to be rough out there. And keep the child away from the edge; we don't want him swept overboard.'

We cleared the estuary and felt the full force of the wind as we sat on some sacking under the bridge. Some charred wreckage floated by - this was no pleasure trip. A damaged destroyer steamed towards us on its way to the dockyard. But there could be no turning back - or could there? The tannoy boomed out: 'This is the Captain. If the weather deteriorates much further, we will have to put back into Liverpool.'

For my part, I had ceased to care. The ferry had begun to roll with the swell. Not just forwards and backwards but side to side - up and down, up and down, side to side. I was sick, very sick, retching again and again. Mother was not, she looked at me with a mixture of sympathy, astonishment and disgust.

A sailor rushed over to us. No mistaking his feelings. No sympathy there - anger, real anger. 'Stop that child. He can't be sick on those sacks. They're full of rabbits. Someone's got to eat those rabbits.'

Too late. No power on earth could stop me being sick then. The sea intervened by breaking right over the bow and drenching us all. It washed away all trace of my crime. The sailor laughed. 'Never mind. We'll feed them to the **** Germans. Hold tight to the stair rail over there and you'll be OK.'

We did. Nothing could have induced mother to sit on a sack of dead rabbits, even if I had not added a distinctive flavour to them.

The ferry ploughed on, making headway against the wind but painfully slowly. The gale increased in intensity. Occasionally, the waves began to wash over the deck. The crew put up storm shutters to help keep the water out, but this meant we could no longer see the waves - and more important, no one could lean over the rail to be sick.

The deck suddenly filled with very sick people doing their best to avoid one another but not always succeeding. We were shut in, a feeling of claustrophobia, of sheer wretchedness - and the stench. Surely matters could get no worse? No. The ferry gave a violent lurch to starboard and came close to capsizing.

The tannoy again: 'This is the Captain. Hold on tight. Do not panic.' We lurched to port and as we did so the ferry staggered under the blow of a huge wave, but righted itself. 'Sorry about that. We've sighted a periscope looking at us a mile to port. I've reported it but the navy has no submarine in the area. We have to assume it's a U-Boat. My orders are to proceed at full speed ahead and steer in random zigzags. In this storm, we will from time to time be broadside to the waves. May God be with us.'

For the first time, mother was sick - she looked ashen. Now, I had to look after her. But there was nothing to be done. We could only sit there on the deck, holding on to the stair rail like grim death and pray.

We never learned whether the U-Boat fired torpedoes at us. If it had, the rise and fall of the swell was so great, they might easily have passed underneath. Then again, we were hardly the biggest fish in the sea.

* * *

We arrived in Douglas, safe but sick and very unsteady on our feet. Father was there to meet us, but not the father I knew. He wore an officer's uniform, complete with revolver in a holster, and he looked very fit - at least two stones lighter than the father who had waived us goodbye in Bournemouth.

Mother rushed into his arms and smothered him in kisses. This really was going to be a second honeymoon for her. Father beamed as soon as he realised we had both come through our ordeal unscathed.

He ushered us away from the ferry terminal, on to a nearly deserted promenade lashed by the wind and sea. 'I've booked us into that hotel,' he explained. 'It's nearly empty. There are virtually no holidaymakers; just a few businessmen.'

We heard the tramp of marching feet. 'Get that child out of the way, sir,' a sergeant yelled. A column of perhaps a hundred men in grey German uniforms marched sloppily down the center of the road, escorted by a British corporal in front, a sergeant in the rear and four soldiers on each side. The soldiers made no attempt to march, but brandished the bayonets on their rifles threateningly at the column. The NCOs both held tommy guns across their chests in the manner of experienced men, who had had battlefield experience and learned to hate Germans.

Mother remarked quietly: 'There aren't enough guards. If the prisoners made a break for it, scores would get away, even though those two do look as if they want to use their submachine guns.'

'Don't worry,' father told her. 'None of those men are Nazis. The Hitler youth aren't allowed out of the camps. Anyhow, we have crack troops no more than five minutes drive away. Commandos training for an operation and then there's my lot.' He did not elaborate and mother winced at the implication.

Over breakfast the next morning, I learned that father had just completed a gruelling officer's training course. 'One of the guys there was a regular, a staff sergeant who had just served three months in the desert and been commissioned in the field. They gave him hell. Now his commission has been confirmed, he'll always be an officer. I helped him through some of the more technical stuff; he gave me a hand on the rifle range by putting three bulls eyes into my target. Told me he had no wish to become a sniper and needed a few weak scores.'

'The course was much tougher in some respects than in peace time, except that everyone who completed it passed. They've stopped making blanks. The machine guns firing low over our heads had to use live ammunition. That really does make you keep your head down.'

He had no idea where he would be posted when he reported back at the end of his leave. When he did learn, it would be secret and he would not be allowed to tell us.

At the end of the week, we wished him luck, and I took a miserable mother home to Pecket Well. The sun shone. The ferry ran to time in a calm sea. Life had to go on.

* * *

CHAPTER 8

Barbarossa

> '- - I see the ten thousand villages of Russia where the means of existence is wrung so hardly from the soil - - I see advancing upon all this in hideous onslaught the Nazi war machine, with its clanking, heel-clicking, dandified Prussian officers, its crafty expert agents fresh from the cowing and tying down of a dozen countries. I see also, the dull, drilled, docile, brutish masses of the Hun soldiery plodding on like a swarm of crawling locusts.' (Churchill's broadcast to the Nation 22nd June 1941).

Barbarossa was Hitler's codename for the planned blitzkrieg against Soviet Russia launched without warning on 22nd June 1941. Despite British warnings, the invasion took Stalin completely by surprise and large numbers of Russian planes were destroyed on the ground before they could take off.

The Germans coordinated their attack in all sectors of the frontier from the Baltic to the Black Sea. The Northern Army Group of twenty nine divisions (three armoured) headed for Leningrad; the Central Army Group of fifty divisions (nine armoured) for Smolensk and the Southern of forty one divisions (five armoured) for the Dnieper. Other divisions were held in reserve and two thousand seven hundred aircraft flew in support, smashing Russian resistance.

The Russians outnumbered their attackers both in the air and on the ground, but their forces were scattered and the surprise so complete that, as in France, German tanks smashed through the defences and within a month had advanced over three hundred miles into the Soviet Union.

However, Russia is not France. Hitler had miscalculated on the considerable resources available to Stalin, and on the willingness of Britain to supply its new ally with scarce war materials. The vast spaces meant that the German tanks had to pause and refurbish worn engines and tracks. Moreover Leningrad and Stalingrad refused to surrender even when surrounded and smashed to pieces.

The Russians suffered brutal atrocities, but this only made them fight to the death with great heroism. And then the winter came and the German army, having assumed the serious fighting would be over before winter, found itself ill prepared for subzero temperatures.

Between June and November 1941, the position of Britain steadily improved. The Luftwaffe suspended its bombing raids both on the United Kingdom and on our forces in the Mediterranean so as to concentrate on smashing Russia. This enabled our armaments factories - with help from America - to reequip the British army with modern weapons and to build up the fighter strength of the RAF. Some of the output of fighters was dispatched to Russia to assist in their resistance.

Equally, the Royal Navy reasserted itself in the Mediterranean, fortified Malta and prevented much needed supplies reaching Rommel and the Africa Corps. In November, General Auchinlech took the offensive in the desert war and for a time relieved the siege of Tobruk. Rommel struck back but was held until on 5th December 1941 Hitler transferred a whole Air Corps from the Russian front to support him.

If only this amelioration in our affairs had continued into 1942, but it did not. Hitler acquired a powerful ally in Japan - not that it consulted him before striking at Pearl Harbour!

* * *

For mother and me, the summer of 1941 was a big improvement on the cold and damp of the previous winter. Grandfather would come at weekends and drive us to the local beauty spots. The views from the moors which crown the Pennines are stunning. In places, you can see for miles with no sign of human habitation - just hills, granite outcrops and heather.

The local farmers graze their sheep on the moors in summer, using sheep dogs to round them up. That summer, one flock from the farm on which we lived had been panicked by a low flying plane and committed mass suicide by bolting over a cliff. The farmer reported his loss to the Ministry of Agriculture who told him not to worry. They would collect the carcasses and have them manufactured into corned beef - a product which formed part of the wartime meat ration.

One evening that autumn, we were disturbed soon after dark by the growl of a mass of low flying aircraft - perhaps thirty or so. German bombers. But what were they doing flying over our hills. We watched intrigued, but not really alarmed. Bombers had flown overhead before, but not for some months.

Suddenly, the sky lit up. They circled and started dropping flares. But surely there was nothing to see except sheep and heather. Mother firmly bolted the door and made me lie under the bed. Were we going to have a raid? No siren had sounded. We had no air raid shelter. Having thoroughly alarmed us, the planes flew on and we thought no more about it.

The following afternoon, father drove up in an army jeep. He wore battle dress and I noticed that his revolver was tied to his wrist by a lanyard. 'Don't you touch that gun,' he warned me, 'it's loaded. I'm not on leave. I'm here on army business.'

He questioned us about what we had seen the previous evening. 'So it's true. We suspected it was a silly rumour. Who runs the Home Guard? They'll have to cope initially, but we'll reinforce them when we know what we're coping with.'

The local Home Guard could hardly be regarded as a serious force. It did have a certain amount of ingenuity. Its principal weapon consisted of twenty or so heavy circular concrete blocks deposited in a line just below the crest of the hill high above the main road to Hebden Bridge. If enemy vehicles attempted to use the road, the idea was to roll the blocks down on top of them and crush whatever got in the way. Father's view of this is unprintable.

'Idiots. We're worried about enemy paratroops landing on the moors where there is absolutely nothing to stop them, and these people think they're playing some kind of glorified marbles.'

He told mother that if the Germans came, she should put the oak dining table on its side against the bed and hide underneath. Then he was gone. You may imagine what this did for our morale. Not much sleep for the next few nights. Then news of a further onslaught on the Russians and we felt safer.

Father's visit did us a power of good with the villagers. A real soldier - an officer. And his family living in our village. Imagine.

The effect on mother and me was rather different. The previous winter in our cold damp cottage had been a miserable experience. The prospect of German paratroopers dropping in force on the moors nearby - as they had done so successfully in Crete in May 1941 - destroyed any illusion that the place was safe. And the bombing seemed to have stopped. How were we to know that this was only a temporary respite?

Moreover, the teachers in the village school advised mother that they could only provide me with a very basic education. That decided her. We would move. But where?

Father was temporarily based at a regional headquarters in Manchester. Mother decided to join him whilst she had the opportunity. Knowing she hated the cottage, he offered to find her a flat and a school for me. Not difficult, Manchester had been heavily bombed and many people had moved away from the centre of the city.

Now, the bombing seemed to have ceased, and my parents had come to believe in father's philosophy of predestination - that if a bomb has your name on it, you are dead whatever you do; and if not, it will miss you. It had made life in the London blitz bearable for him and he had survived it with little more than a scratch.

James Lingard

Early in 1942, father's army life allowed him to have the occasional day off - no parachute landings; no bombs. Even so, Manchester had considerable strategic significance and there had to be troops in the area to defend the city.

Before the war, Victoria Park had been one of the more pleasant residential areas, but a bomb had destroyed one of the grand houses and people had moved away. We took a flat nearby in a small block finished just before the war and still not fully occupied. No Anderson shelter, but that was a plus point as far as we were concerned.

On any Saturday that father had leave, we would visit Withenshaw, which then had a park with a vast expanse of grass and rhododendron bushes. I have no idea why the grass had not been ploughed up and planted with vegetables. 'Dig for Victory'. Today, both Victoria Park and Withenshaw are large council estates!

Now, I had grown out of Toy town, but the BBC had a new appetiser broadcast before the six o'clock news. 'Dick Barton Special Agent' could be relied upon to start every fifteen minute episode by escaping from impossible odds, but to end it in even greater danger. He was, of course, a winner. In a world of censorship, that had to be the perceived destiny of our Nation.

For school, I obtained a place at the preparatory school for William Hulme's Grammar School. This had not been evacuated, but remained at its original site in the city. I had to change buses to reach it, but having been shown how to get there for the first week, the exigencies of the war made it necessary for me to travel there and back - complete with gas mask - by myself from the age of seven.

People had a great patriotic spirit; we were all in it together against the Germans. Crime existed - particularly a black market to mollify rationing - but to a far less extent than now. Murderers were hanged; mugging was risky - too many citizens had military training, some like father carried guns and knew how to use them.

Sadly, the cessation of bombing proved to be temporary. On the 23rd April 1942, the Luftwaffe started night time meaningful bombing of British cities once again. But now, the Americans had begun to arrive and we were able to retaliate. On 30th May, the allies launched the first one thousand bomber attack on Germany, devastating Cologne. The Germans persisted and on 26th July the RAF heavily bombed Hamburg.

I remember one particular raid on Manchester. The bombing had not been particularly close to us; as always, the censored news downplayed its severity. Mother decided that I should go to school as normal. She did take me to the stop for the first bus to see if it was running normally, and when it came waved me goodbye.

I alighted as usual to find a long queue for the second bus. The usual passengers were astonished to see me. 'There's been a raid. Didn't you know? But his parents will have gone to work, he'd better go on.'

Eventually, a bus came. The top deck had been smashed in by a bomb but the lower deck remained serviceable apart from cracked windows. 'Come on,' the lady conductor called. 'We'll take as many of you as can cram on board. Nobody upstairs, it's not safe. To hell with the regulations. This is war.'

The school made our education as normal as possible. In the circumstances they did a fantastic job and we all tried our hardest. Rationing had kept us fit, no overweight children in those days. Moreover, we lived in a harsh world of death and destruction - no one had 'human rights' or the expectation that the State would provide for them.

* * *

CHAPTER 9

The Americans Declare War

**'Not once or twice in our rough island story,
The path of duty was the way to glory.' (Tennyson)**

The winter of 1941/2 saw a series of disasters for the Allies, despite having four fifths of the world's population on their side. On 7th December 1941 came the Japanese attack on Pearl Harbour, wiping out all but two battleships in the American Pacific fleet. Fortunately, the aircraft carriers were at sea. Hitler had no advance warning and was as astonished as the rest of the world.

The very next day, Japanese forces landed in Malaya, Thailand and the Philippines and three days later Burma. Manila fell on 22nd December, Hong Kong on 25th December, Kuala Lumpur on 11th January and Singapore on15th February 1942.

The defence of Singapore proved to be a complete shambles - the Australian Prime Minister described it as an 'inexcusable betrayal'. Britain sent men and ships but the Japanese overwhelmed the fifty or so Hurricane fighters. We had too many problems in too many places and our priorities lay nearer home. The defenders outnumbered the invaders, but had been taken by surprise at the speed of the Japanese advance and were completely disorganised. We had lost control of both air and sea - the Japanese could reinforce at will.

Why did the Japanese believe they had any chance of success? We had done our best to keep secret the horrendous losses our navy had suffered. The Bismarck had sunk HMS Hood - one of our newest battle cruisers - on the 24th May 1941, before being sunk herself three days later.

Then, on 13th November the aircraft carrier HMS Ark Royal was sunk off Gibraltar by a German submarine, followed a fortnight later by the loss of HMS Barham, a battleship. Shortly after Pearl Harbour, the Italians using midget submarines crippled the battleships HMS Queen Elizabeth and HMS Valiant and a British cruiser squadron ran into a German minefield with heavy loss. Suddenly and unexpectedly, we had lost control of the Mediterranean, having only three cruisers and a few destroyers left there in serviceable condition. The Germans could now reinforce Rommel and they did so at will.

Even worse, on 10th December, the Japanese air fleet, fresh from its success at Pearl Harbour, found and sank the battleships HMS Prince of Wales and HMS Repulse off the east coast of Malaya. They now had control of the Pacific, and China had all but collapsed. Surely, the Far East was theirs for the taking?

British concern centered on the Atlantic and the need to protect our vital supply conveys not only from the ever present U-boats but from powerful German surface raiders. By the end of 1941, the Germans had a U-boat fleet of approaching two hundred and fifty, of which over one hundred were operational at any one time. They created havoc, particularly near the American coast where the convoy system was not yet in operation.

The battleship Tirpitz - the most powerful ship then afloat - stationed at Trondheim in Norway from early in 1942, made it necessary for the British Home fleet to comprise at least two King George V battleships and an aircraft carrier.

The battle-cruisers Scharnhorst, Gneisenau and escorting cruiser Prinz Eugen had refitted in Brest. They had the speed to outrun our battleships, long range firepower to outgun our cruisers and successfully tied up our remaining capital ships.

On the evening of 11th February 1942 under cover of darkness, the German squadron in Brest successfully jammed British sea-watching Radar and slipped out into the Atlantic, where they joined a powerful force of escorting destroyers. Hitler had decided to leave the Atlantic to his U-boats and concentrate his capital ships on stopping supplies from the West reaching Russia. He also had an obsession that we intended to retake Norway.

Many years later, I learned what happened to the Brest fleet from a naval commander who was awarded the Distinguished Service Cross. He spent most of the war in command of a motor torpedo boat patrolling the English Channel and western approaches and fighting the enemy E-boats. These were larger and more heavily armed, but slower than the British vessels. Both sides usually patrolled in packs - whichever was the stronger force would chase the other off.

On the morning of the 12th February, he was returning to base from a routine patrol, the sea calm but some mist and fog and no other ship in sight. There had been air activity over the French coast but nothing to trouble him. No warning of enemy aggression.

The mist began to clear as the winter sun rose and he became aware of smoke on the horizon heading directly towards him from the Atlantic. Probably a convoy, but he had not been briefed to expect one. He became aware that the ships were approaching at speed. Must be naval vessels. He contacted base, but they were mystified. He received orders to investigate.

Action stations. He set off at speed towards the smoke, but two German destroyers headed in his direction and opened fire. Time to break off, but he had seen the two dreaded battle-cruisers in the distance and radioed their precise position to Portsmouth. His orders were now to shadow the enemy but keep out of range. The RAF confirmed the sightings, but were driven off by Messerschmitts.

The unequal confrontation lasted fully two hours as the enemy had the audacity to head up the Channel towards Dover. His fuel was running low, but mercifully he was told that units of the Home Fleet had left Portsmouth and would be joining him shortly. When they opened fire, he was to report the fall of shot, until notified that they could see the enemy themselves and he was no longer needed.

Unfortunately, none of the King George V battleships were in Portsmouth and the British fleet in its weakened state found itself outgunned. The Germans forced their way right through the Channel and out into the North Sea. The heavy batteries at Dover opened up but missed their target. Six torpedo carrying fleet air arm Swordfish attacked the Germans, but all were shot down. Motor torpedo boats, destroyers and such other units of the fleet as could keep up with them attacked but seemingly to no avail. In fact the Gneisenau suffered such heavy damage that it took no further part in the war. The Scharnhorst also suffered damage but was back in service six months later.

The incident had a considerable affect on the public's moral. Were the Royal Navy's losses such that it had lost control of the Channel? We all knew that the press was censored. What would happen if the Germans assembled another invasion fleet? The Americans had not yet arrived. Would they come or were they totally committed to defending themselves against the Japanese?

* * *

CHAPTER 10

1942

> 'We are resolved to destroy Hitler and every vestige of the Nazi regime. From this nothing will turn us - nothing. We will never parley; we will never negotiate with Hitler or any of his gang. We shall fight him by land, we shall fight him by sea, we shall fight him in the air, until, with God's help, we have rid the earth of his shadow and liberated its peoples from his yoke.'
> (Churchill's broadcast to the Nation 22nd June 1941).

By the middle of 1942, things should have been improving. We were no longer fighting alone against overwhelming odds. The enormous armies of Russia and of the United States of America were both on our side, yet everywhere the Allies were in full retreat. The German blitzkrieg against Russia had slowed but by no means been checked. The Japanese were still advancing and now threatened both India and Australia, depending on the direction they chose to take.

Britain continued to pour much needed supplies into Russia via the Artic convoys. In March 1942, German aircraft and U-boats began seriously to threaten those convoys. The battleships Tirpitz and Scheer and the cruiser Hipper were also in Norwegian waters where they would have been joined by the Scharnhorst and Gneisenau but for the damage inflicted upon the two battle cruisers in their dash through the English Channel.

At the beginning of July 1942, the Admiralty believed the German fleet had sailed to intercept convoy PQ17 and ordered the thirty four merchant ships to scatter. As a result twenty three were sunk by enemy submarines and aircraft. This disaster led to the Artic convoys being suspended until September and then again until December, resulting in problems for the Russians. Despite all their efforts, Sevastopol on the Black Sea fell on 2nd July 1942 and the Germans reached Stalingrad on the 24th August.

The U-boats in the Atlantic had great success in the first half of 1942, sinking over three million tons of merchant shipping, mostly close to the American seaboard before the US organized an effective convoy system. By July, the fifty lend-lease American destroyers were escorting allied convoys and the losses halved. The destroyers were old and relatively slow, but faster than any merchant ship.

A naval officer who spent his war on convoy duty told me of an incident when the elderly lend-lease US destroyer on which he served was dive bombed in the western approaches to the English Channel. The ship was equipped with anti-aircraft batteries on each end of the bridge. One of the gunners who opened up on the dive bomber kept on firing as it swept across the ship, causing all the officers on the bridge to throw themselves flat to avoid their heads being shot off. 'Just one of the teething troubles in fighting an unfamiliar vessel!'

The Japanese continued their onslaught, aiming first to take Ceylon and eventually India. The Dutch East Indies were quickly overwhelmed, the Americans were forced to yield the Philippines on the 22nd March 1942, Mandalay in Burma fell on 31st May and the Japanese landed on Guadalcanal on the 7th July.

The British made frantic efforts to provide fighter aircraft to defend Ceylon from the expected onslaught, the carrier Indomitable ferrying in aircraft as fast as she could. A British naval force also arrived there on 24th March comprising the battleship Warspite, four old battleships, three aircraft carriers, seven cruisers and sixteen destroyers. Would this be enough?

On 4th April 1942, a large enemy force was reported approaching Ceylon, but the British reconnaissance aircraft was shot down before she could supply details. The following day, eighty Japanese dive bombers struck Colombo, but British fighters were waiting and twenty one of the attackers were shot down. The attacking force in fact comprised the ships which had wrought so much damage at Pearl Harbour. Most of the British fleet was at sea and lucky to escape.

The strength of the fighter resistance surprised the Japanese and fortunately they did not press ahead with their attack, preferring to refit their fleet. They had in fact already achieved their original objectives, but with such unexpected ease that they were tempted to expand even further.

Meanwhile, the British seized Madagascar from the Vichy French to strengthen the allied position in the Indian Ocean. More important, the Americans sent two of their latest battleships to reinforce the British Home Fleet. A start had been made in replacing the heavy naval losses we had suffered earlier in the year.

Britain at War 1939 to 1945

The Japanese turned their attention to Australia and sent two aircraft carriers with supporting escort to attack Port Moresby on the south coast of New Guinea. The Americans also had two carriers in the area and on the 6th May 1942, the battle of the Coral Sea began. The losses of both sides were roughly even, but the Lexington sank whereas the heavily damaged Shokaku and the invasion fleet made it back to base. The other carriers remained battle worthy.

The Japanese decided to take Midway Island from which they could threaten Hawaii and Pearl Harbour itself. The battle of Midway began on the 3rd June 1942. The Japanese had a strong force of four aircraft carriers and eleven battleships, three of which were amongst the most modern then existing. The Americans could only deploy three aircraft carriers - no battleships - but they had the airstrip on the island, as long as they could hold it from the landing force.

The initial attack on the airstrip was repulsed with heavy casualties on both sides. A counter strike on the enemy fleet was driven off by carrier born fighters. But then planes from the US carriers surprised the enemy. From the first wave of forty one torpedo bombers, only six returned; then a second wave hit and knocked out three of the four Japanese carriers for the loss of a further twenty five planes. The fourth carrier countered and sank the Yorktown but was itself sunk in turn. The battle fleet could still have taken Midway, but now lacking any air cover chose to retire under cover of darkness.

Midway represented the first clear defeat for the Japanese, but they were by no means finished and set about establishing themselves on Guadalcanal in the Solomon Islands. They were dislodged from the airbase on the 7th August but two days later surprised and sank four allied cruisers, disrupting allied attempts to reinforce. Seventeen thousand US marines were left ashore without air cover to face strong Japanese reinforcements.

Somehow, they stuck it out. Fierce jungle fighting punctuated by screaming bombs and the ear splitting explosion of naval shells continued until 9th February 1943 when the Japanese finally withdrew. They had lost one carrier, two battleships and four cruisers against allied losses of two carriers and eight cruisers. American naval losses in the Pacific were now so substantial that they were sent the British carrier HMS Victorious to provide additional air cover.

The Japanese then attempted to take Port Moresby in New Guinea, defended by Australian troops newly returned from fighting in the Middle East. The attackers crossed the Owen Stanley Mountains and landed some troops from the sea, but their convoys carrying reinforcements were attacked from the air and suffered crippling losses. One convoy estimated to be transporting 15,000 troops was totally annihilated. The Australians held; the Japanese died in their thousands - many from starvation and disease - only a few hundred survived.

* * *

In order to mount an invasion of Europe or to continue supplying arms to Russia, the Allies needed control of the Atlantic. The U-boats had been taking a dreadful toll - supplemented by surface raiders and magnetic mines - up to 1943, and it became a priority to curb the menace. Sinkings had exceeded impressive new construction by seven million gross tons. The Americans had the arms and the men but they needed to be brought to Europe.

By March 1943, over 100 U-boats were constantly on patrol in the Atlantic and sinkings in the month rose to 540,000 tons. This was crisis level. But two technical developments saved the day. Very long range Liberator aircraft based in Newfoundland and Iceland became able to give daylight air cover to the Atlantic convoys the whole way across to Britain, forcing the U-boats to stay underwater. Secondly, the British developed new short range radar to install in the aircraft which the submarines could not detect. Moreover, the Allies at last had sufficient destroyers to form attack groups independent of the convoys.

In March / April 1943, 27 of the 235 U-boats then in action were destroyed in the Atlantic - a considerable improvement on earlier efforts. Allied shipping losses fell by nearly 300,000 tons. In May, U-boat losses rose to 40 and by June, some convoys began to come through intact with total losses for the month at less than 30,000 tons. A real achievement for the new tactics.

The German discomfort was increased further when the British fitted flight decks for naval aircraft to nineteen of their larger merchant ships. These aircraft now took the offensive when a U-boat was sighted.

* * *

CHAPTER 11

The Desert

> '- - We have lost upwards of fifty thousand men, - - - a great mass of material, and, in spite of carefully organised demolitions, large quantities of stores have fallen into enemy hands. Rommel has advanced nearly four hundred miles through the desert, and is now approaching the fertile delta of the Nile. - - - We are at this moment in the presence of a recession of our hopes and prospects in the Middle East and in the Mediterranean unequalled since the fall of France.'
> (Winston Churchill on the fall of Tobruk 2nd July 1942)

Early in 1942, Britain was not under direct threat, but Churchill felt the need to demonstrate to our Allies that we were doing all in our power to support them, particularly after the capitulation of Singapore and the problems we were having with the Artic convoys to Russia. He had, therefore, built up our forces in Egypt and pressed for them to advance across the desert. Here, our strength was at least equal to the Axis powers and he looked for a victory.

Rommel was not prepared to wait. The horrendous losses suffered by our Mediterranean fleet had enabled him to be resupplied and on the 26th May he ordered the German Afrika Korps into action. Fierce fighting raged for a week with losses estimated at 350 to 400 tanks and approximately 170 aircraft on each side.

Then, a British counterattack failed with further heavy losses.

Worse, the 15th and 21st Panzer divisions swept into the desert, around allied lines and attacked from the rear. Disaster. Allied forces withdrew in some disorder. The supply base at Tobruk was supposed to be held at all costs; but once surrounded, it quickly surrendered on the 21st June. The Panzers had outgunned and destroyed large numbers of British tanks. Indeed, the 4th armoured brigade was reduced to a mere twenty tanks - all the Allies possessed until the reinforcements speeding towards Egypt arrived.

The British retreated to Mersa Matruh where they were joined by a New Zealand division, but all were driven back to El Alamein - only forty miles from Alexandria - despite strenuous resistance by the New Zealanders and RAF fighter cover. Here, the Quattara Depression prevented the Germans from outflanking the Allies, but Rommel had been considerably strengthened by the supplies captured at Tobruk.

* * *

From July 1942, allied reinforcements began to pour into the desert. The 8th Armoured Division with 350 tanks quickly followed by two infantry divisions materially strengthened the defence. But we were no longer fighting alone. The Americans also intervened, sending three hundred of their latest Sherman tanks and a hundred 105-mm self-propelled guns, weapons equal to any the Germans had in the desert.

James Lingard

Both sides saw Malta as a key to the desert. When operational it could effectively prevent Rommel being reinforced. Equally, without it, the British fleet no longer controlled the Mediterranean. But the island was under constant air bombardment and running out of food and ammunition.

On 9th August 1942, the Allies made a desperate attempt to resupply Malta. A battle fleet of two battleships, three large aircraft carriers, seven cruisers and thirty two destroyers entered the Mediterranean to escort fourteen of the fastest merchant ships available and the carrier Furious all loaded with supplies.

Two days later, the position of this force was identified by a German submarine which sank the carrier Eagle. However, the Furious successfully flew off the squadrons of spitfires she was delivering to Malta. Then the air attacks on the convoy started and the battleships withdrew. 39 enemy aircraft were shot down - in addition to 13 destroyed by Malta based fighters - but enemy U-boats and E-boats joined in.

Only three of the merchant ships reached Malta under their own steam, two others including a vital American oil tanker were rescued and towed in. Their cargoes proved sufficient to rearm the spitfires, the Island quickly became fully operational again and Rommel's supplies suffered accordingly.

On 13th August, General Auchinlech was replaced as Supreme Commander in the Middle East. He had been outmaneuvered by Rommel and had become too defensive, being reluctant to move troops out of Syria in case the Germans drove south out of Russia and attacked the oil fields in Iraq and Iran. He need not have worried, the Russian defence held - even Stalingrad, though almost totally destroyed, never surrendered. The Germans failed to force their way across the Caucasus.

General Montgomery took command of the 8th army and resolved to hold the Alam el Halfa ridge until all his reinforcements had arrived and made themselves ready to take the offensive. Rommel attacked on the 30th August, adopting his usual tactic of sending the 15th and 21st Panzer divisions around the desert flank of the British forces with a view to hitting them from the rear. This had been anticipated and they ran into strong British armoured divisions which stood their ground and forced them to a standstill. The Germans dug in and awaited a counterattack. The Allies did not oblige but stayed put. Eventually, the Panzers had to withdraw and Rommel used them to form a strong defence at El Alamein.

Only on the 23rd October 1942, when all preparations had been completed, did the Allied counterattack commence. By then, the Commonwealth forces had assembled over a thousand tanks, half of them American Grants or Shermans equal in quality to those of the enemy. The RAF had attained a fighting strength of 550 aircraft in the desert and at least as many more to harry Rommel's supply routes.

This time, the Qattara Depression ruled out any possibility of an allied flanking attack and the Germans had laid deep minefields and built strong anti-tank and machine gun positions. They had, however, only 240 serviceable tanks and had lost control of the air. Montgomery launched a frontal attack, but only after an artillery barrage from a thousand guns had prepared the way. The battle raged for twelve days and ended with the total defeat of Rommel's army. By 5th November, he could only muster thirty eight tanks to fight a rearguard action as he withdrew westwards in the direction of Tobruk.

The defeat of Rommel at El Alamein in November 1942 was the first important allied victory of the war. We had been encouraged by news that the Russians then the Americans had joined us in the struggle, but in both cases our new Allies had immediately suffered colossal disasters. Could anyone stop a blitzkrieg, or the savagery of the Japanese? Now, at last, after three years of war, the Panzers had been stopped. Now, hope of victory returned.

* * *

The Allies maintained their pressure - not only the eighth army which pursued the retreating Germans and recaptured Tobruk on 12th November; but on 8th November the Americans launched an invasion of French North Africa led by General Eisenhower. This achieved complete surprise; the Germans were fooled into believing that all the preparations at Gibraltar were for another Malta convoy. At the request of President Roosevelt, the operation had been kept secret from General De Gaulle, which had an adverse effect on future relations with the French.

The Vichy French resisted invasion, particularly the landings in Morocco, Algiers and Oran, but the battleships Massachusetts and Rodney with supporting

Royal Navy units silenced the coastal batteries and on 11th November, the Vichy leader in North Africa surrendered to the Americans. Hitler immediately retaliated by ordering the occupation of Vichy France, but failed to capture the fleet at Toulon which scuttled itself in the harbour.

The Germans acted promptly to counter the invasion, diverting reinforcements originally intended for Rommel to Tunisia. By the end of the month, they had assembled 15,000 front line troops supported by 100 tanks, artillery and dive bombers. But the price of redeploying a quarter of the German air force to the Mediterranean was that 400 planes had to be diverted from the Russian front. This proved a serious mistake.

Hitler flew in his elite paratroops - by December German strength had risen to 50,000. The build up continued whilst Eisenhower was prevented from pressing home his attack on Tunis by torrential rain and poor roads. Rommel continued to fall back on Tunisia. On 23rd January 1943, the British eighth army captured Tripoli. A few days later, his retreating forces joined up with the Axis troops defending Tunisia and on 14th February he became able to mount a counterattack.

The allied forces encircling the Germans were too thinly spread, enabling the striking force of two Panzer divisions to break through. Fortunately, they then struck north towards the coast where they were held by the 1st Guards Brigade. Other allied units came up and after fierce fighting the Germans withdrew, but fighting continued for many weeks.

General Alexander took command of the front in the last week of February and expressed himself shocked at the situation which he found. He regrouped his forces.

General Montgomery only had transport to advance part of the eighth army into Tunisia and realised that Rommel would counterattack his units. He therefore took up defensive positions around Medenine and on 6th March successfully beat off four major counterattacks by all three available Panzer divisions, destroying 52 tanks by gunfire. Rommel was invalided back to Germany three days later.

The Germans retreated into strongly fortified positions around Mareth. These were only overwhelmed after heavy air attacks and seven days of heavy and continuous fighting on the 28th March. A few days later the British and American armies linked up and began the final siege of Tunis.

The Germans endeavored to supply their troops by air but suffered such horrendous losses that the attempt had to be abandoned. On18th April, 100 transport planes were intercepted by spitfires and American fighters and more than half were destroyed. Similarly, at sea 137 Axis supply ships were sunk together with 21 escorts.

The main attack on Tunis commenced on 22nd April 1943. The Germans eventually surrendered on the 13th May when the Allies took nearly a quarter of a million prisoners and captured over 1,000 guns and nearly 250 tanks many of which were still serviceable.

The Allies estimated that the North African campaign as a whole cost the Axis powers 950,000 men killed or captured (many of them Italian); 2,400,000 tons of shipping sunk; 8,000 aircraft destroyed; 6,200 guns; 2,550 tanks and 70,000 lorries - a heavy loss indeed to Hitler and his cause.

Perhaps Hitler would have done better to concentrate his efforts against the Russians? They too were beginning to see some success. On 31st January, Field Marshal Paulus had been forced to surrender the Sixth German Army which had attempted to take Stalingrad with the loss of twenty one German Divisions.

A proud Churchill sent Stalin a copy of the film 'Desert Victory'. Stalin was suitably impressed and ordered it to be 'widely shown in all our armies at the front and amongst the widest masses of our population'.

* * *

CHAPTER 12

Russia

> '- - The series of prodigious victories which tonight brings us the news of the liberation of Rostov-on-the-Don leaves me without power to express to you the admiration and the gratitude which we feel to the Russian arms.' (Winston Churchill to Stalin 14th February 1943)

By the spring of 1943, the immense power of the Russian army began at last to force back the German onslaught all along the line from Leningrad in the north to Rostov in the south. Stalingrad had refused to surrender to enormous pressure from the German Sixth Army, but by January 1943 the Red Army counterattacks had reached within ten miles of the besieged city. The Germans fought desperately, but by the end of the month were forced to surrender. The Sixth Army was no more; the Russians had 90,000 prisoners.

Equally, the Germans were forced back from their investment of Leningrad, another city which had heroically resisted every effort to storm it, its starving citizens fighting on passionately in the ruined streets through the bitter winter. The Red Army rolled on - Rostov on the 14th February; Kharkov two days later.

But the Germans were not yet finished. They sent a powerful battle fleet comprising Tirpitz, Scharnhorst, Lutzow and supporting destroyers to Narvik and forced the allies to suspend their Russian convoys during the daylight of the summer months, materially weakening the Soviet effort. On 5th July 1943, the Germans counterattacked the Russian salient around Kursk with their new Tiger tanks, but the initiative had been expected and they were driven back. Kharkov was only finally liberated on the 23rd August 1943.

Moreover, that summer the Russians achieved air supremacy due to Hitler withdrawing fighters to bolster his position in North Africa and to defend against Western bombing. The Germans attempted to hold the banks of the Dnieper but to no avail. Kiev was liberated on the 6th November 1943. Stalin's troops had advanced more than two hundred miles that summer. Then on 11th April 1944, the German army in the Crimea was cut off and the Russians set about recapturing Sebastopol which was liberated on the 9th May 1944.

Hitler still had two hundred divisions on the Russian front, but he made no attempt to regroup them. Their orders were to stand and fight - another mistake; a recipe for disaster.

The artic convoys resumed in November, the Tirpitz having been disabled by a daring attack by miniature submarines. She was subsequently sunk by the Royal Air Force. The December convoy was challenged by the Scharnhorst, but she was surprised and sunk by the British flag ship HMS Duke of York and her escorting destroyers. No German battleships now remained to threaten the artic convoys or to break out into the Atlantic. Victory in the northern oceans had at last been achieved.

The Artic convoys supplied Russia with 5,000 tanks and over 7,000 aircraft. After the heavy losses suffered in 1942, the convoys sailed only in the dark winter months and achieved considerable success in boosting the weapons and ammunition devoured by the Soviet forces.

* * *

The Russian offensive in the summer of 1944 was an unqualified success. Viborg in Finland surrendered on 21st June after twelve days of hard fighting and the railway from Murmansk to Leningrad was reopened a few days later speeding supplies to the stricken city. Finland surrendered to the Allies on 25th August.

The attack on the central Russian front began on 23rd June - Stalin's way of supporting the D-Day landings in Normandy - and in the following five weeks the Germans retreated 250 miles, liberating the whole of the USSR. Twenty five Nazi divisions ceased to exist and a further twenty five were cut off.

In July, the Russians broke through the German lines in the south and poured into Poland, stopping short of Warsaw to resupply and reorganise - to the distress of the Polish resistance who had risen up prematurely on 1st August and were massacred. Unfortunately for them, the Hermann Goering Panzer Division - a crack unit - had recently arrived from Italy supported by two other S.S. tank divisions equipped with the latest Tiger tanks.

Further south, the German defence of Rumania and its oil fields held until the middle of August but was then destroyed with the loss of a further sixteen Nazi divisions. Bulgaria was overwhelmed; Stalin reached the Yugoslav border and turned up the valley of the Danube towards Budapest and Vienna, pausing to consolidate and resupply only at the Hungarian border. In three months of summer, German losses on the Eastern front had reached crippling proportions.

The Russian advances came close to cutting off the German garrisons in the northern Baltic States and in Greece, but they were skillfully extracted and Hungary reinforced. The Russian advance began again on 6th October aimed at Budapest. Belgrade fell on 20th October, its German garrison annihilated, but Budapest held out with six weeks grim street fighting through January.

Although the Germans resisted valiantly in Hungary, Warsaw fell on 17th January 1945 and the Russians swept through Poland, across the German border into Upper Silesia and headed for Danzig - which, however, held out stubbornly. By the end of January 1945, the Nazis had virtually been forced back into Germany and Northern Italy. The Allies set about bombing the railway system out of existence.

* * *

CHAPTER 13

Italy

'The time has come for you to decide whether Italians shall die for Mussolini and Hitler - or live for Italy, and for civilisation.' (Allied leaflet dropped on Rome 17th July 1943)

After the conquest of North Africa, the Allies decided to strive for Sicily and if this proved feasible, the Italian mainland. This required 3,000 ships / landing craft to transport 100,000 men with tanks, guns and equipment - no mean undertaking. The British Eighth Army under General Montgomery comprising seven divisions, two armoured brigades and commandos was to seize the east of the island; whilst the U.S. Seventh Army under General Patton comprising six divisions took the west.

Against them stood two German divisions - one of which was armoured - and four Italian divisions supported by local troops. Similarly, the Allies could muster 4,000 operational aircraft, whilst the Axis powers had less than half that number in the region.

The well prepared offensive was launched on the 3rd July 1943 with an intensive air strike which quickly established air superiority and kept the Italian navy away from the invasion fleet. Four transports were sunk by German U-boats but the landings were successfully accomplished on the 10th July. The only disaster befell the Air Landing Brigades whose gliders were cast off too early and became scattered with many casualties.

The German Panzers launched a heavy counterattack against the Americans; German paratroops brought in from the mainland slowed the British advance. However, the Allies brought up further divisions held in reserve and by the 17th August, Sicily had fallen. Many of the German troops succeeded in withdrawing during the night across the Messina Straits to the mainland, but there were 37,000 German casualties and over 130,000 Italian. It became clear that the Nazis were not popular with the Italian population.

* * *

The landings in Sicily had serious political repercussions in Rome. Italy itself now faced the threat of invasion. Mussolini fell. He was arrested on the 25th July 1943 on the orders of the Italian King following a vote of the Grand Council, and interned on the island of Ponza. A substantial majority of the population of Italy had turned Communist virtually overnight. Communist demonstrations were put down by armed force.

The Germans poured men into Rome, backed by an armoured division on the outskirts. The Italian troops in the vicinity had practically no weapons. The King and Italian Government were forced to pretend support for Hitler but requested the Allies to land in Italy at the earliest opportunity. The Allies requested that the Italians order their air force and fleet to leave the country and surrender, release all prisoners of war and destroy communications in the north to disrupt any German invasion.

Hitler, however, ordered reinforcements into Italy and the country rapidly came under German occupation. The Italian Government signed an armistice surrendering to the Allies on the 3rd September 1943. Before dawn that same day, the British Eighth Army had crossed the Straits of Messina and landed on the toe of Italy.

During the night of September 7th, the Germans encircled and subsequently seized Rome but the King and senior ministers escaped to allied occupied Brindisi. That same day, the Italian fleet escaped from its bases to Malta and surrendered with the loss of the flagship Roma sunk by German aircraft. Hitler responded by sending in paratroops to rescue Mussolini and set him up as a rival Government on the shores of Lake Garda in North Italy. There, he remained cut off from the outside world by carefully chosen German guards.

The Italian surrender and the relative speed with which Sicily had been liberated encouraged the Allies to proceed with the invasion of Italy. However, there were sixteen German divisions stationed in Italy; eight in the north under Rommel, two in and around Rome and six in the south under Kesselring. Moreover, twenty German divisions had been withdrawn from the Russian front and were refitting in France. The Allies had control of the sea and air, but not enough troops on the ground to ensure success and not enough landing craft to bring in massive reinforcements.

* * *

On September 8th, the Allies landed at Salerno, south of Naples, under cover from a strong British fleet but without much air support as the fighters were at the limit of their range. The Germans had disarmed the Italians in the vicinity and put up a strenuous resistance. Salerno itself fell, but the Herman Goering Armoured Division based in Naples, the 16th Armoured Division and a regiment of the 1st parachute division backed by support from the Luftwaffe contained the landing within a ten mile perimeter. For six days of bitter fighting the issue remained in doubt. Naval bombardment saved the Allies from being pushed back into the sea, but at the cost of the battleship Warspite being disabled by a glider bomb - one of the new German secret weapons.

However, the landing did disrupt the German defence of Italy and on the 9th September the Royal Navy steamed unopposed into the naval base at Taranto in the heel of Italy and landed six thousand men of the British 1st Airborne Division who seized the port. This enabled much needed allied reinforcements to be landed.

By September 16th, the danger of defeat at Salerno had passed. Elements of the British Eighth Army fighting its way up from the toe of Italy began to arrive and the Germans had to withdraw to meet this new threat. Naples itself fell a few days later and within two weeks its harbour had reopened and its airfields became bases for Allied fighters.

Once Naples had been taken, the Allies advance met increasing resistance and of necessity paused. The Germans now had nineteen divisions ranged against no more than thirteen. Reinforcements had become a necessity. They were available but landing craft had other priorities as well. The shortage of transports prevented the relief of Rhodes and other Greek islands which remained under Nazi occupation.

* * *

On the 12th October, the Allies resumed their advance, but early in November they came upon the forward defences of Hitler's main strategic position south of Rome which had been strongly reinforced. The opposing armies were of equal strength and the Germans had orders not to withdraw from the mountainous defences which they held. They had been told that if they held out, the new secret weapons now developed would destroy London and force the British to seek an armistice.

Moreover, the Allies began withdrawing troops and landing craft back to England to prepare for the invasion of France. That invasion had absolute priority - indeed the existence of the secret weapons made any delay risky. The result in Italy was a deadlock for a period of severe fighting. This suited the Germans well enough - the divisions they held in reserve could be made available at short notice where needed, be it Russia or to repel an invasion of Northern France.

The stalemate was no use to the Allies. They needed Rome to convince neutrals such as Turkey that they were now winning the war. They needed the airfields north of Rome to bomb industry in Southern Germany, and Stalin needed to prevent reinforcement of the Nazi armies in Russia. But how to break the stalemate? Frontal assaults proved costly and were only partially successful.

Allied landing craft were about to be withdrawn from the Mediterranean but Churchill saw the opportunity to land two divisions at Anzio, just south of Rome, behind the German lines. Would two divisions be enough? There were not enough transports to land more.

The landings on 22nd January 1944 achieved almost complete surprise, but the advantage failed to be pressed home. The road to Rome was open but the troops were held back to Churchill's fury. Worse, German reserves quickly came up and sealed off the bridgehead. Then, they launched a heavy counterattack on 16th February narrowly failing to drive the Allies back into the sea - repulsed by bombardment from every aircraft the Allies could fly.

The Allies resumed frontal attacks on Monte Cassino, but during winter and early spring this resulted in heavy casualties and precious little progress. It did, however, cause the Germans to commit reserves and pinned down nearly twenty good divisions weakening their efforts against Russia.

* * *

Once the snow on the mountains had melted and the ground hardened, the Allies were able to attack on a much broader front in support of the D-Day landings in Northern France. In great secrecy, they had used the spring to regroup and reinforce their forces in Italy.

They now mustered twenty eight divisions against the Germans twenty three and had succeeded in concealing the point of attack.

The fresh onslaught started at 11pm on the 11th May 1944 when 2,000 allied guns opened up a barrage followed up at dawn with heavy bombing. The Polish Corps once again tried to take Monte Cassino but yet again were repulsed. The French Corps made some progress into the mountains and after thirty six hours of murderous fighting the Germans began to fall back. The Americans attacked in strength up the coast road, but it took a week before Cassino town finally fell.

German reinforcements now began to arrive. Would they make a stand in the Alban Hills / Valmontone just south of Rome? They tried to hold a line along the river Liri some miles to the south but the Canadians broke through on the 24th May and that triggered the six allied divisions now in the Anzio bridgehead to break out. German losses were heavy, but the crack Hermann Goering Panzer Division was on its way south to stop the rot. It arrived at Valmontone before the Americans and held the main road open to allow the retreating German units through.

The Alban Hills held out for a few days but Rome fell on the 4th June - two days before D-Day and the Normandy landings. The Germans fell back to the mountains north of the city where the terrain made things difficult for the allied armoured divisions. The retreat, harassed by air attacks, was disorganised and closely pursued by the Allies.

Kesselring reorganised his forces to hold a strong prepared position named the Gothic Line which ran across Italy along the Apennine range north of Florence. There his retreating army would be reinforced by eight new divisions. He skillfully fought rearguard actions to slow down the advance.

General Alexander, on the other hand, had to release seven divisions - almost 40% of his troops - to take part in the landings in the south of France. The strategy agreed by the Allies was to tie up Nazi strength in Italy rather than conquer territory in the mountains. Churchill tried his hardest to keep the troops in Italy to continue their advance, notwithstanding the Gothic Line. Fortunately, the Americans and the Russians forced him to stand by the agreed strategy. The advance through France proved far easier and less costly in lives.

The attacks on the Gothic Line continued but heavy casualties were sustained. The German strength was reinforced to twenty eight divisions and held with the aid of the weather into the winter. Churchill asked the Americans to send reinforcements to Italy, but they declined - sending them instead to strengthen the armies on the Rhine. The mountains of Italy led back to the Alps - territory far too easy to defend and costly to attack as had been proved at Monte Cassino.

* * *

CHAPTER 14

Far East

'--Forward, unflinching, unswerving, indomitable, till the whole task is done and the whole world is safe and clean.' (Churchill speaking on the surrender of Germany)

1943 saw much hard jungle fighting by the Australians and Americans as they slowly - over a two year period - drove the Japanese out of New Guinea and the Solomon Islands. The Huon peninsular in New Guinea held out against the Allies for five months, at the end of which two thirds of the Japanese defenders were dead. The liberation of New Guinea effectively ended the threat to Australia and New Zealand, both of which had initially seemed at risk.

Air power dominated the struggle, and by the summer of 1943 Japanese losses in the air exceeded those of the Americans by four to one. Their base at Rebaul in New Britain continued to hold out, but the Americans swept round it and by March 1944 had captured the whole of the Admiralty Islands. Island after island in the Central Pacific began to fall to the Allies as the United States regained naval ascendancy, but many were stubbornly contested by troops who refused to surrender.

The Japanese began to concentrate their efforts on a land invasion of India through Burma. The Allies were heavily pressed on other fronts and had far less experience in jungle fighting as events in Malaya had shown. Wingate led airborne troops into Burma to cut Japanese communications and disrupt their supplies. Although initially successful, he died in an air crash on 24th March 1944.

On 8th March, three Japanese divisions began their assault on the Imphal plateau just inside the Indian border. A month later, the advance was held back at Kohima, but by May they had surrounded sixty thousand British and Indian troops on the plateau, troops who could only be supplied by transport aircraft withdrawn from the campaign in Italy. The monsoon rains threatened to disrupt supply. Then on 22nd June 1944, a British relief column fought its way through from India and the Japanese began to withdraw with heavy losses.

Fighting continued despite the monsoon rains - the Japanese Fifteenth Army was shattered, having lost 65,000 men from death, disease or hunger. The British and Indians continued a slow painful advance with the aid of air support against increasingly stiff resistance until the rains became so heavy that operations squelched to a halt.

General Stilwell in the north of Burma strove to link up with a Chinese army advancing from Yunnan province. The land route to China finally reopened in January 1945, but Japanese pressure on China forced Chiang Kai-shek to withdraw his best divisions. Moreover, transport aircraft and landing craft required for an attack on Rangoon were needed in Europe. Mandalay was eventually captured on 20th March

1945; Rangoon not until 3rd May - just as the monsoon started in earnest. By then, Hitler was already dead!

Churchill wanted to restore British prestige by retaking Singapore via Burma and Malaya, but America had different priorities, preferring to seize the Philippines and island hop to Japan. All agreed that the United States were in command in relation to the Japanese war. And the Japanese? They sent a powerful fleet including seven battleships to Singapore. Who could tell where they would target next?

* * *

At the end of 1942, the Americans had been short of aircraft carriers and even had to borrow the carrier HMS Victorious from Britain. They set about mass producing basic new carriers and achieved the astonishing rate of one a week.

The destruction of the Tirpitz and Scharnhorst enabled the British to reconstitute a Far Eastern fleet. By April 1944, three battleships, two carriers and a strong flotilla of submarines had been transferred to Ceylon, reinforced by the US carrier Saratoga and the French battleship Richelieu. That summer, they began to make their presence felt and gradually severed the ability of the Japanese to supply Rangoon by sea. By November, they had been joined by the latest battleships HMS Howe and HMS King George V. The Japanese in Burma - and their prisoners - began to starve.

By June 1944, the American island hopping was approaching the Philippines. The Japanese fleet had withdrawn from its base at Truk but when the US threatened to take Guam, it decided to strike. Japan needed a decisive victory at sea to survive. On 15th June, the Americans sighted a fleet of five battleships and nine carriers heading in their direction and lay in wait with fifteen of their carriers.

On 19th June, Japanese planes attacked from all directions but were decisively defeated in the all day air battles, forcing the fleet to withdraw. In the ensuing pursuit, three Japanese carriers were sunk before the fleet escaped, but Guam fell - and Guam was within bombing range of Tokyo.

The High Command in Tokyo brought up reinforcements from Manchuria and ordered a fight to the finish by their army and a final attack by their entire fleet. The American attack on the Philippines commenced with air raids on 10th October 1944, persisted in for most of the following week, by when Japan's air force was smashed before the naval engagements had even begun.

On 20th October, General MacArthur landed four divisions on Leyte in the Philippines and found resistance weak. A decoy fleet sailed direct from Japan - its carriers weakly equipped but its purpose to entice away the US fleet. Meanwhile, the main Japanese striking force from Singapore and a second battle group from the south made for the American held landing beaches.

The Americans located and repulsed the Singapore fleet which turned back, its heaviest battleship sunk. They then located and set out in pursuit of the decoy force. But the main Japanese striking force swung round and resumed its original target. The battle group from the south was repulsed, but the US had no effective answer to the Singapore fleet which sank the carriers protecting the landings. Inexplicably, it did not make the most of its advantage but withdrew. Had it bombarded the beaches, the Allies might have suffered a serious reverse.

After the above naval battles, the conquest of the Philippines proceeded very much to plan. The Japanese tried desperately to defend Manila - losing 16,000 dead in the process - and held on for a few months, but with no real prospect of success.

By March 1945, the British fleet in the Pacific had finally built itself up to attack readiness. The battleships HMS King George V and HMS Howe with four fleet carriers having a complement of 250 planes supported by five cruisers and eleven destroyers bombed islands south of Okinawa on the 26th March. Four American divisions landed on Okinawa - an island stubbornly defended by over one hundred thousand Japanese troops. The Japanese fleet tried to intervene, but on 7th April was virtually destroyed by an American carrier force.

The Japanese then resorted to kamikaze suicide attacks - launching over 1,900 such attacks before Okinawa finally fell on 22nd June. Ninety thousand of the Japanese defenders were reported to have died.

The British attacked again in May and bombarded the island of Miyako. This time, the suicide bombers severely damaged the carriers HMS Formidable and HMS Victorious, but their armoured decks saved them from destruction.

Meanwhile, the Australians landed in Dutch Borneo and subsequently took Brunei and Sarawak. There remained the Japanese mainland, defended by a well equipped army of over a million fanatically pledged to fight to the death. But then, the Allies had a secret weapon of their own.

* * *

CHAPTER 15

D-day

> 'In wartime, truth is so precious that she should always be attended by a bodyguard of lies.'

The Allies had long agreed that the invasion of Northern France must have priority over all else - other operations in the Mediterranean were all secondary. The Russians, of course, regarded the defence of their country as paramount, but Stalin offered to time his next offensive to assist the invasion - in fact attacking in strength on the 23rd June 1944. The Americans also gave priority to the landing over their operations against the Japanese in the Pacific. By D-Day, 1.5 million US troops were stationed in Britain; troops who ridiculed British deference to concepts of class and the old school tie.

As a preliminary to D-Day, 6th June 1944, the French railway system suffered heavy bombing to disrupt German communications and reinforcements. Meanwhile, elaborate planning struggled to work out how best to transport 150,000 men and 20,000 vehicles to France in the first two days and how to convince the enemy that the attack would be directly across the Straits of Dover. This subterfuge, involving erecting dummy tanks guns and vehicles in the Kent countryside, was brilliantly successful and resulted in Panzer divisions being held back from the actual landings.

The invasion force comprised thirty five divisions carried in 4,000 ships supported by 11,000 aircraft of which 8,000 would go into action. In the early hours of D-Day, three airborne divisions landed behind the invasion beaches. They had mixed success: some of the gliders being blown off course; some landing too close to enemy strong points.

As dawn broke, the huge invasion fleet began its attack. German torpedo boats sank a Norwegian destroyer. An expected attack by U-boats was beaten off by aircraft which sank six of them.

The day yielded thousands of heroic actions. As an illustration, I tell that of Maurice Bennet, a civilian who had joined the Royal Naval Volunteer Reserve on the outbreak of war, and three times set out in capital ships to escort convoys to Malta. All three times, his ships had been disabled by torpedoes or bombs and with difficulty limped back to Gibraltar. When the North Africa campaign drew to a close, he had volunteered to command a tank landing craft, and successfully participated in the landings at Salerno before being ordered back to the UK in order to participate in the D-Day landings.

He and another officer volunteered for special duties. Could any such duty be more dangerous than driving a cumbersome landing craft on to a heavily defended beach? Well - yes.

Maurice was to command a landing craft modified to contain one tank and three guns - all with their barrels in fixed positions to fire straight ahead at a target one thousand yards away. He had orders to search out a

James Lingard

shore battery; aim the guns by steering straight at it, then fire at 1,000 yards.

D-Day dawned and Maurice and his sister craft went in at full speed ahead - such as their craft could manage - well ahead of the invasion fleet. The beach had been heavily bombed, but it seemed as though they were alone against the might of an invisible German army.

A mile out and no target identified. Suddenly, a loud explosion to port. A quick glance - the sister ship had received a direct hit and exploded into pieces. Zigzag. Just in time. Another battery closer to Maurice fired at him. This is it. He headed directly for it. Hold on - 1100 yards. Wait for it - fire.

Maurice and the battery fired more or less simultaneously. They missed; he did not. The shell from the tank hit the concrete bunker, but made precious little impression on it. The shells from the three guns exploded - - and produced red smoke. Red smoke, Maurice swore as he turned away from the beach to try another attack.

Suddenly, a tremendous explosion. The battery had gone - not only the battery but the low cliff on which it stood had collapsed into the sea.

Time to take on the second battery which had sunk his sister craft. Maurice had to cover half a mile before he was in range. Random zigzags and a lot of prayer. They fired but he made it. Once again red smoke; once again a huge explosion and the battery had half gone.

He received a signal: 'Leave immediate'. No need to be told twice. He turned back out to sea - a sea now covered with scores of ships. As he did so, he saw the flash of heavy guns - a Rodney class battleship firing another broadside at the remains of the battery.

Could there be any survivors from the sister craft? Another signal: 'Get out of the *** way.' Dozens of landing craft were powering directly at him on their way to the beach and glory. He made it back - many of the others did not.

* * *

Generally, the Allies achieved complete tactical surprise, but on Omaha beach, the Americans ran into a full German division on the alert and had great difficulty in achieving a landing at all. Elsewhere, resistance proved to be lighter than expected - smashed into submission by the naval bombardment and the heavy bombing which effectively destroyed the German radar.

By nightfall on D-Day, 150,000 Allied troops had landed at a cost of approximately 10,000 killed. The Allies hoped to reach Caen, a few miles inland, but this was prevented by a force of fifty Panzers.

Inevitably, the early days after landing had times of chaos and improvisation. An infantry Colonel told me how his regiment rapidly fought their way out of the landing zone and into the Normandy countryside. Three days later, they had achieved their immediate objectives but had had no sleep and precious little food. No Germans in sight. He called a halt, requisitioned a convenient farm house as temporary headquarters, put his men into defensive positions and posted sentries.

James Lingard

He instructed his sergeant major that they were all exhausted and would fight better after a few hours rest, but he was to be called if any German troops were sighted. With which he threw himself on top of a bed. Too hot; he took his uniform off, but adhered to standing orders and left his loaded revolver, safety catch on, tied to his wrist with a lanyard.

The next thing he remembered was that the sergeant major burst into the room, shook him roughly by the shoulder, yelled: 'Quick, sir. The Germans are surrounding the house.' flung open the window and jumped out.

Had he dreamed it? He heard a voice shout in German. Hell. No time to get dressed. He flung himself through the open window and landed on his feet, just as two German soldiers came round the corner. They stared at the near naked man in astonishment. He fled for the further corner of the building, but as he ran jerked the revolver into his hand.

He heard a shouted challenge and in reply fired two rapid shots, hitting one of the soldiers in the arm. They returned fire but he was round the corner. A burst of fire from the sergeant major's tommy gun and both Germans were dead. A quick dash to the nearest hedge, and there were a Company of his regiment lying in ambush. The Germans withdrew as rapidly as they had arrived.

In another sector of the battlefield, a bridge building unit had strict orders as to precisely where to bridge a canal which threatened to hold up the allied advance. They drove directly to the map reference - no sign of military activity in the vicinity.

Within a few hours the bridge was completed ready to be tested. The colonel always insisted on being the first to drive across and this he did. Still no sign of allied tanks - he reported the position and was ordered to sit and wait for them.

Suddenly the roar of engines and twenty Panzers quickly surrounded him and his men. They were disarmed and the German commander told him that they had been watching him for the past hour and his bridge would be most useful.

Three of the German tanks escorted the unit to a German base ten miles or so to the rear. There the British officers were entertained to dinner in the officers' mess, while the men were marched off to another building.

Half way through the meal, a knock on the door and a British colour sergeant entered and saluted smartly. 'A problem, sir,' he said to the Panzer major. 'May I have a word with my colonel?'

Permission was readily given and the colonel walked over to the door. 'The men are getting restless,' he was told. 'We have overpowered the handful of men guarding us and taken their weapons. There is a guard on the gate and four German officers with you, but that's all. The tanks have gone. Permission to carry on, sir?'

The colonel consented and within moments the tables were turned and the bridge building unit drove out of the camp with four Panzer officers as their prisoners. They headed back towards their bridge. Two miles short of the bridge, they entered the square of a small town, and to their horror saw the Panzer tanks which had captured them. These were drawn up in a neat row with their crews sitting on or around them, relaxing and drinking beer.

They heard the tank engines starting up as they raced on. The colonel radioed his Head Quarters for help. They made the bridge in record time and raced across. The colonel jumped out to lay a charge and dynamite it. An American voice came over the radio: 'Don't do that. Let them come. We're waiting for them. Just get lost will you.'

The unit sped on under no illusion that next time the Germans would not be so gentlemanly. Then, behind them gunfire erupted. A tank battle had begun; the Panzers had been ambushed. The colonel did not wait to see who won.

* * *

Heavy German reinforcements were hastening to the front, but equally the Allies planned to have twenty five divisions deployed within a month. The sixty German divisions - of which ten were Panzers - available to defend France against the invasion were widely spread around the coast; only nine infantry and one Panzer being on hand in Normandy. Such had been the success of the allied deception that they planned to attack Calais.

By 12th June, the Germans had brought four Panzer divisions into the battle - less than General Eisenhower expected. The air offensive had succeeded in disrupting communications. Cherbourg held out until the 26th June and the port suffered heavy demolition which put it out of action for a further ten weeks. The weather also deteriorated and storms destroyed one of the two floating harbours which had been towed across the Channel. Even so, good progress was made in supplying and building up the bridgeheads.

As in Russia, Hitler made the mistake of ordering his troops to stand and fight where they were, rather than making strategic withdrawals. In the last week of June, the British front was attacked by strong Panzer forces, but they were beaten off with heavy losses by air attack and accurate artillery fire. On 8th to 10th July, a British counterattack at last succeeded in taking Caen which had suffered heavy bombing.

By mid-July the Allies had thirty divisions ashore opposed by twenty seven German divisions weakened by heavy allied bombing whenever the weather permitted. Rommel himself suffered severe wounds from a low flying fighter. The Nazis could only respond at night with attacks by single aircraft. Then, on 20th July 1944, desperate anti-Nazis attempted to assassinate Hitler, but failed - leading to a massive purge which included Rommel himself.

Hitler now released his Fifteenth Army to oppose the landings, but their intervention came too late to make much impact. The American break out under General Bradley began on the 25th July and cut the German escape route down the Normandy coast. Four Panzer divisions checked the Canadian advance on Falaise. Brest on the tip of the Cherbourg peninsular held out until the 19th September.

Hitler insisted on a major counterattack by five Panzer divisions on Mortain but this was beaten back. Much of the surviving armour succeeded in withdrawing before the gap in the allied advance at Falaise closed, but eight German divisions were effectively annihilated.

The allied advance continued and on 24th August entered Paris. The Germans are estimated at this stage to have lost 400,000 men - half prisoners - and 1,300 tanks.

* * *

CHAPTER 16

The Battle For Europe

> 'You may rest assured that we shall do everything possible to render assistance to the glorious forces of our Allies.' (Marshal Stalin to Churchill)

On 14th August 1944, allied forces landed in the South of France in a number of places along a stretch of coast between Toulon and Cannes. The landing craft hit the beaches under cover of a substantial naval bombardment provided by six battleships and twenty one cruisers with supporting destroyers. The Allies also had total air supremacy and had bombed the fortifications in the area for the previous fortnight.

American and British paratroops dropped around Le Muy to cut German communications and seize the pass through to St Tropez. They were quickly joined by the seaborne forces. Shortage of landing craft restricted the initial attack to commandos and three American divisions, but they were quickly followed by seven French divisions.

The Germans had withdrawn four of their divisions to support the defence of Normandy. Ten divisions remained but only three were in the vicinity of the landings and they had also to deal with 25,000 men of the French Resistance who had been resupplied by the Allies.

Marseilles and Toulon were left to the French divisions and held out to the end of the month. Meanwhile, the Americans drove north reaching Grenoble on August 24th and Lyons on September 3rd. The only serious opposition came from a Panzer division at Montelimar north of Avignon, but they were driven back by heavy air attacks. The French Resistance liberated Dijon on September 11th and on that same day, the allied forces which had landed in the south met those from Normandy. Less than a month after the landings, the Germans were in full retreat leaving behind over 50,000 prisoners.

* * *

Meanwhile, General Eisenhower took command of the allied forces in France on 1st September 1944 - thirty seven divisions comprising over half a million troops. The Germans opposed them with about seventeen divisions, harassed continuously by overwhelming air power. The Allies urgently needed a port to ease their stretched supply lines and advanced as fast as possible. The Guards Armoured Division covered 200 miles in four days - Antwerp was taken on the 4th September before the Germans had carried out demolition of the harbour facilities.

However, resistance stiffened as the Allies neared the German border. There, they came upon the Siegfried Line - a long prepared defensive position. Any further advance only came after much hard fighting. Unfortunately, the Nazi strength was seriously underestimated in intelligence reports. The parachute drop to seize the bridge over the Rhine at Arnhem launched on 17th September ran into a Panzer division and failed with the loss of 7,500 experienced troops. The bridge over the Waal at Nijmegen was, however, taken and held despite German attempts to destroy it.

During October, the Allied advance paused whilst strenuous efforts were made to capture the strongly held Scheldt estuary, which barred the access of shipping to Antwerp. After heavy bombing and bombardment, the Germans eventually succumbed to courageous Commando attacks in the first week in November. The first convoy began to unload supplies on the 28th November amidst a deluge of flying bombs and rockets which caused many casualties.

Early December 1944 found the Allies stuck on the German frontier, still well short of the Rhine. Equally, they remained stuck in Italy where the Germans still retained twenty six divisions, and the weather negatived allied superiority in armour and in the air. The situation in Burma, where weakness forced Chinese forces to withdraw, was no better. The Americans, however, were making progress in the Pacific; as were the Russians on their front.

But Hitler had been regrouping his forces for a counterattack. No fewer than seventy divisions - fifteen of them armoured - faced the Allies on the Western front. A seventy five mile sector in the Ardennes, from Bastogne in the south to Malmedy in the north, was relatively weakly held by four US divisions. On 16th December, under cover of a heavy artillery barrage, the Germans launched ten Panzer divisions supported by fourteen infantry divisions against them, and inevitably broke through the allied lines. Could they swing north and recapture Antwerp thereby depriving the Allies of much needed supplies?

In the north of the salient, the Sixth Panzer Army met advancing detachments of the First US Army and were held for some days in fierce fighting around St Vith by the Seventh US Armoured Division. However, the Fifth Panzer Army brushed aside the forces opposing it and headed for the river Meuse.

General Eisenhower stopped all allied attacks and committed all his reserves - some sixteen divisions - to defend the northern flank of the salient and prevent the Germans reaching the coast. Hitler's forces penetrated some sixty miles towards the Meuse, but on 23rd December, the weather improved and the Allies launched heavy air strikes with considerable effect. The attack faltered and switched to Bastogne where the US 101st Airborne Division had held out. They continued to hold against all the odds.

On 1st January 1945, the Luftwaffe launched a heavy surprise attack on all allied forward air bases and did substantial damage. But then, General Montgomery in the north and General Patton in the south attacked the salient simultaneously, whilst the Russians brought forward an offensive they were planning on the eastern front.

The forces north and south of the salient struggled through snow storms until they met at Houffalize on 16th January. The Germans were squeezed back to their frontier with casualties of 120,000 men - losses they were unable to replace.

* * *

CHAPTER 17

The Home Front

'The nations not so blest as thee
Must in their turn to tyrants fall;
While thou shall flourish great and free,
The dread and envy of them all.'
(Chorus to Rule Britannia)

By the start of 1944, the war situation was improving. News bulletins were in general more optimistic. In particular, the horrendous threat of invasion had gone; American forces were arriving in numbers and making their presence felt. Moreover, bombing raids on Britain had tailed off. The RAF had command of the skies.

The mighty German army had been driven out of North Africa and the Allies had captured Southern Italy. The Russians had begun their unstoppable advance, and the Royal Navy had sunk the last German battleship. The Americans were beginning to reclaim the Pacific Islands - though the situation in Burma was still a cause for concern. The allied invasion of Northern France could not be far away.

But life remained a struggle. Every family had someone at the front or at least in harm's way and casualties continued to be high. Rationing had become more severe than ever. New improved U-boats - one of Hitler's much vaunted secret weapons - had become available to continue the struggle in the Atlantic. There were shortages of nearly everything - rationed or not - caused by the Limitation of Supply Orders designed to divert production to war work. The winter blackout induced a misery of its own.

Clothes were now rationed, but not blackout material. Good quality clothes surprisingly took no more coupons than cheaper equivalents. The Government had introduced well designed Utility clothes in September 1942; then Utility furniture, but furniture was only available for people who were bombed out or newly married.

Then in May, the allied forces broke the German defences at Monte Cassino in Italy and on 6th June 1944 came the D-Day landings in Normandy which everyone had been expecting. Could this be the beginning of the end? US Flying Fortress bombers based in England continued to carry out devastating daylight bombing raids on Europe. On 13th February 1945, Dresden was destroyed in a fire storm which killed at least 50,000 people. The pressure on Hitler was mounting.

The news of the invasion evoked a huge wave of emotion and patriotic fervor. General Eisenhower broadcast not only to the nation but to the world. Occupied countries were told to be patient, 'we are coming'. Even music on 'Worker's Playtime' - normally continuous in the factories - was interrupted for the announcement of the landings.

Any thought of celebration soon subsided. The landings were heavily opposed; casualties were high. Then on 13th June, German bombs again fell on London. No aircraft; just a large bomb - one ton of high explosive. A new secret terror weapon which

Hitler called the V1 because it was the first in a new series of horror weapons planned to smash Britain's will to continue the fight.

Over three thousand V1 rockets were launched against Britain in the next five weeks, killing or maiming over 2,000 people and destroying or damaging thousands of houses. The bombardment lasted until the middle of September. Too late; the launch sites fell to advancing allied troops. In all, 2,400 of the 8,000 or so bombs launched hit their target, killing 6,000 and seriously injuring 18,000. Many bombs were destroyed before they could be fired.

Some mothers and children were again evacuated. The bombs flew at three thousand feet at approximately four hundred miles an hour - too fast for most fighters then in service, but not the latest planes in specially stripped down form. In addition, anti-aircraft guns were moved to the coast to counteract them.

The engines of the V1 made a loud distinctive buzzing sound, and stopped when so instructed by a propeller set to measure the distance from the launching site. Whilst the noise continued, people were safe. When it stopped, you knew the bomb was falling and had seconds to throw yourself flat to evade the blast. You could tell the direction it was travelling, but not how far it would carry before exploding - and the explosion was massive. The rockets flew at all times of day or night, whatever the weather, and imposed even more stress than traditional bombing.

* * *

The elimination of the V1 threat by the advancing troops brought only temporary relief. Hitler followed it up by launching the V2, an even more formidable terror weapon. This took the form of a rocket with a range of 200 or so miles and again a one ton warhead. The Germans were able to produce about 600 a month from September 1944 to March 1945.

The V2 made no warning engine noise, but exploded with an earsplitting thunderclap and vivid blue flash. When fired, it rose to a height of fifty miles and fell at a speed of 4,000 miles an hour. Once launched, it was unstoppable and its victims never knew what hit them. The crater was often 50 feet wide and ten feet deep, and the force sufficient to destroy a row of terraced houses. About 1,300 were fired at Britain, killing 2,724 and seriously injuring 6,476. Even more V2s terrorised Belgian cities after they were liberated.

The real terror of the V2 was that no one knew when or where it would fall. Anyone could die at any time. Now was the time to believe that if a V2 had your name on it, you were dead; and if it did not, you would live another day.

By the winter of 1945, nearly half the houses in the London area had been destroyed or damaged. Bombed sites were everywhere - properties with boarded up windows and tarpaulins for rooves in bitterly cold conditions. People were war weary. Now the danger had passed, strikes started to add to the misery - strikes often over petty grievances of little real concern to anyone.

In the closing stages of the war, the advancing Americans discovered large stores of rockets near

Leipzig. The Germans were also developing multiple long-range artillery to blast London into submission. The war ended just in time to prevent horrendous carnage and damage; but then, the Allies had a massive secret weapon of their own as the Japanese were to discover.

* * *

CHAPTER 18

Victory

> '- never have the forces of two nations fought side by side and intermingled in the lines of battle with so much unity, comradeship, and brotherhood, as in the great Anglo-American Armies.'
> (Churchill's Victory Broadcast)

Despite defeat in the Ardennes, Hitler decided to resist the Allies west of the Rhine, instead of using the river as a shield. Both sides fielded approximately eighty two divisions, but many of the enemy troops lacked battle experience and they suffered from allied bombing, lack of air support and particularly from shortage of petrol. The ten Panzer divisions of the Sixth Army had left for the Russian front to try and save the oil fields. Stalin's offensive had weakened the German defence on the western front as he had promised.

Field Marshal Montgomery advanced on the Rhine north of Cologne over sodden ground, but met strong defences and determined resistance. It took until the 10th March 1945 to drive all eighteen German divisions opposing him back across the river. They left behind 53,000 prisoners and many dead.

Further south, General Bradley proceeded more rapidly, captured Cologne on 7th March without too much difficulty and found the railway bridge over the Rhine at Remagen damaged but still usable. Four allied divisions were quickly across; General Patton's forces came up and the Germans lost a further 40,000 prisoners immobilised by lack of petrol. Patton then swept down the Rhine behind the Siegfried Line and captured its garrison. The Rhine was also crossed south of Mainz, and a second bridgehead formed threatening Frankfurt which was captured on the 29th March.

The allied air forces kept up a sustained attack on German airfields. This became essential; the Germans had invented and brought into service a new jet fighter, faster than any we had. Fortunately, their production lines had suffered in the bombing - the threat dwindled away.

Meanwhile, Field Marshal Montgomery set about crossing the Rhine in the north, close to the industrial heartland of the Ruhr. Capture or isolate the Ruhr and Hitler would be finished. Kesselring had now been put in command of the defence and he brought with him seven divisions of crack paratroops backed by strong artillery. The Allies proceeded to weaken the opposition by heavy bombing, and strafing by no fewer than 3,000 fighter aircraft.

Allied forces crossed the river at night on the 24th/25th March to find the far bank only lightly defended. This initiative was followed by parachute landings behind the German lines. In the next four days, a substantial bridgehead had been established with twelve bridges thrown across the river. Troops poured across; the Ruhr itself remained in German hands, but its 325,000 defenders were soon surrounded as the German front collapsed.

* * *

Senior German Generals - but not Hitler - now saw defeat as inevitable. Moreover, the advantages of surrendering to the British and Americans rather than the Russians became obvious to them. They still had 147 divisions opposing the Red Army even when their western front began to crumble, yet they made no attempt to transfer any of these to the west. This naturally annoyed Stalin and prompted a rift between the Allies.

Relations had already become strained because the Russians refused to allow non-communists to take part in the newly constituted Polish Government. Equally, Stalin had not interfered when British troops suppressed a communist uprising in newly liberated Greece. The Russians regarded this as the deal which had been negotiated at Yalta, but Britain had declared war in the first place when the Germans invaded Poland and had always insisted on free elections there. The concept of free elections meant something different to Stalin, who favoured a one party state.

Negotiations with the Russians became complicated by the unexpected death of President Roosevelt on 12th April 1945, just as the war in Europe reached its climax. President Truman, who succeeded Roosevelt, endeavored to continue the same policy as his predecessor, but he did not have the same personal relationship with Stalin.

* * *

As the British and Americans crossed the Rhine, the Red Army overcame the fierce German counterattacks launched against it following the capture of Budapest on 15th February. They advanced up the Danube, taking Vienna on 13th April. In the north, they encircled various strong points - such as Konigsberg - and reached the river Oder, a mere thirty five miles from Berlin. But the banks of the Oder were strongly held by Nazi troops determined to defend their capital from falling to the Russians.

General Eisenhower, for his part, encircled the Ruhr and drove forwards, crossing the river Elbe near Magdeburg on 12th April - sixty miles from Berlin - and taking Leipzig and on into Czechoslovakia by the 19th.

Stalin began the attack on Berlin with massed forces along a 200 mile front on 16th April and by the 25th had surrounded it and met up with elements of the US First Army. The main allied forces halted on the banks of the rivers Elbe and Mulde - Russians to the East; Americans to the West. Eisenhower suspected that Nazi extremists might try to hold out in the mountains of Bavaria and sent strong forces down the Danube, where they met the Red Army advancing up from Vienna at Linz. The German Army now ceased to exist, over a million prisoners surrendering by the end of April.

On the Italian front, the Allies spent the winter months of 1944 reorganising and resupplying - particularly with artillery shells - but used their thirty to one air superiority to disrupt German communications. Hitler had twenty seven divisions - four of them Italian

- against twenty three allied divisions drawn from all over the world, including Brazil. He forbade his men to retreat and thereby robbed them of the strong defensive positions available north of the river Po.

After mass allied air attacks on the 9th April, the British Eighth Army attacked northwards near the Adriatic coast east of Bologna, whilst the Americans attacked to the west of the city which fell after heavy fighting on the 21st. Once the Allies held the river Po, the Italian partisans rose on 25th April and seized Milan, Venice and Genoa. Mussolini was captured and shot by the partisans on the following day. The Germans surrendered in Italy to Field Marshal Alexander and the war in Italy finally ended on 2nd May.

Meanwhile, in Berlin Hitler had shot himself on 30th April, quickly followed by the suicide of Goebbels and later by that of Himmler. Germany finally surrendered unconditionally on 9th May 1945.

After the allied invasion of France, the U-boats became much less effective, despite the German invention of a new type fitted with Schnorkels enabling them to stay submerged and achieve a high submerged speed. They failed because heavy allied bombing prevented sufficient numbers being produced and put into service.

781 U-boats were destroyed during the war, but even so when Germany finally surrendered, forty nine were still at sea and 320 others either surrendered or scuttled themselves. The new boats were one of the secret weapons which encouraged Hitler to carry on fighting to the bitter end. The German capital ships had all been sunk - many by heavy bombing. At the end

of the war, only three cruisers and fifteen destroyers remained of the Nazi fleet.

* * *

Churchill had promised that he would call an election as soon as Germany was defeated. In view of the recent death of President Roosevelt and the need to reach agreement with Stalin on the boundaries and constitution of post war Europe, any change in the British Government could hardly be in the national interest. Nevertheless, on 23rd May 1945, Churchill resigned; the Government of National Unity ended and was replaced by a Caretaker Government of Conservative Ministers until a General election could be held and the votes counted. All concerned agreed that the result would be declared on the 26th July.

In view of Stalin's treatment of Poland, Churchill considered it essential to maintain strong forces in Europe to prevent the Red Army seizing too much territory and imposing communism on reluctant populations. The Americans had little sympathy with such thoughts and were quite content to make concessions to the Russians who had suffered so greatly and contained, then defeated, huge Nazi forces. Moreover, their priority had to be the defeat of Japan. To that end, Truman began to withdraw forces - particularly aircraft - from Europe. Equally, Soviet troops began preparations to attack Japan by moving to the Far East over the Trans Siberian railway.

The result was that a Conservative Government took the hugely unpopular step of delaying demobilisation of forces surplus to military requirements. How could this be justified to a population which had already celebrated victory and which remembered with admiration the heroic defences of Leningrad and Stalingrad? The Russians were seen as our Allies, not our enemies. The British people wanted a Government which could work for peace - not fall out with Stalin - and accordingly they voted for Attlee and a Labour Government to the astonishment of the Conservatives.

* * *

There remained Japan with its kamikaze fanatical military. All the planning revealed that many many lives would be lost trying to subdue such a well armed enemy. Then, as the allied leaders met at Potsdam to discuss the future of the world on the 17th July 1945, they learned that the atomic bomb had been successfully exploded in the Mexican desert and that the results were truly awesome - complete devastation within a one mile circle and massive damage beyond that.

All were agreed that the bomb must be used and a net saving of life would result. On the 26th July, the Japanese were invited to surrender. They declined. On 27th July, eleven Japanese cities were warned that they would be subjected to intensive bombing. Next day, six were attacked. Then, twelve more were warned; four bombed.

The first atomic bomb annihilated Hiroshima on 6th August 1945; the second Nagasaki on 9th August. Japan agreed to surrender on the 14th August and the formal surrender was signed on 2nd September when the Allied fleets had sailed into Tokyo Bay. The war was over at last.

* * *

Epilogue

The introduction briefly touches upon the effect of the First World War on Britain. The effect of the Second World War was quite different, though - just as before - people were worried about unemployment and having somewhere to live. Then again, how would returning troops be received by the families from whom they had been separated?

This time, women as well as men had perished in the blitz - and a number had left the country to marry Americans. The disparity in the number of eligible men and women was far less than in 1918.

In 1947, 22% of married women and most single adult women were in paid work. They now began to demand equal pay, though to this day they still commonly receive less for much the same work.

The Commonwealth had made great sacrifices in Britain's hour of need. Now they demanded and in most cases were granted independence. The loss of India in particular meant that Britain could never again match the power of the United States, though it is taking our leaders a long time to recognise the harsh reality that once again our armed forces have dwindled to a fraction the size of those of several other nations.

Three million houses and other buildings had been destroyed - half in London - and emergency steps had to be taken to clear the bomb sites and provide prefabricated bungalows for people to live in and resume their lives. This time work did exist for the returning troops. Only one in four houses was owner occupied.

Moreover, a Labour Government with a 146 seat majority pursued a policy of social justice. The class system, which had been much derided by visiting American troops, was gradually replaced by a system which rewarded merit - though it has still not entirely disappeared.

Britain had spent her riches and found herself hugely in debt, particularly to the United States. This debt has only recently been finally paid off. The burden resulted in high taxes and greatly impoverished the nation.

On a more personal level, returning troops were entitled by law to be reinstated in their old jobs - that is if their employers still existed. This was not easy after years away fighting a brutal enemy. Soldiers trained to kill had to exercise great restraint if embroiled in a pub brawl. Too often they found that men who had been their junior but had avoided military service were now in senior positions. However, enlightened employers ensured that returning troops were rapidly promoted once they had become accustomed to civilian life.

The war had ended, but rationing and shortages continued into the 1950s - even bread became rationed. Moreover, two years national service in the armed forces remained compulsory for men; one of the reasons why life remained disciplined.

How else did life differ from that we know today? A far higher proportion of couples married, as opposed to simply living together. Divorce and bankruptcy carried a stigma, as did homosexuality.

The concept of human rights was unknown - the victims of concentration camps could vouch for that. Murderers were hanged; delinquents could be beaten. Certainly, recalcitrant schoolboys were in real danger of being caned. Today, even convicted criminals and those who spurn their duties to society are accorded human rights! Is this progress?

* * *

About the Author

I was educated at Dulwich College and subsequently at University College London where I obtained an LL.B. (Hons) degree.

After qualifying as a solicitor - with honours - in 1956, I became a partner in what was then a small city firm, before joining Norton Rose in 1972. There, I specialised in banking law and set up an insolvency practice.

I wrote Lingard's Bank Security Documents (Butterworths) - a leading work in its field now in its 4th edition – Corporate Rescues and Insolvencies (Butterworths) and Tolley's Commercial Loan Agreements. I also gave numerous lectures and wrote for technical journals.

I served for a number of years as a Council Member of the Association of Business Recovery Professionals and of the European Association of Insolvency Practitioners (now known as Insol Europe) - being the first English solicitor to do so. I also became the Chairman of the Joint Insolvency Examination Board and of the Banking Law and the Insolvency Law Sub Committees of the City of London Law Society.

On retirement from practice, I was appointed a judicial Chairman of the Insolvency Practitioners Tribunal and wrote 'Cauldron of Hate' published by Vanguard Press, an imprint of Pegasus Elliot MacKenzie Publishers Limited.

Printed in the United States
112882LV00003B/76-81/P